Let's Wake Up, Italics!

Manifesto for a Glocal Future

 ₋etti

JOHN D. CALANDRA ITALIAN AMERICAN INSTITUTE
QUEENS COLLEGE, CITY UNIVERSITY OF NEW YORK

First published in Italian as

Svegliamoci italici! Manifesto per un futuro glocal
Venice: Marsilio, 2015

English Translation by Gail McDowell

Studies in Italian Americana
Volume 12

ISBN 978-1-939323-08-8
Library of Congress Control Number: 2016948026

John D. Calandra Italian American Institute
Queens College, CUNY
25 West 43rd Street, 17th Floor
New York, NY 10038

Al mio Carleu,

per le troppe ore sottrattele

TABLE OF CONTENTS

PREFACE

Italics of the World, Unite!
You have nothing to lose....

FRED L. GARDAPHÉ

Queens College, The City University of New York

> "Ethnic memory is ... or ought to be
> future, not past oriented."
> Michael M.J. Fischer

In an earlier publication, Piero Bassetti, a veteran in Italian business and government, developed the notion of Italicity by reminding us that:

> we live in a world in which each one of us has a plurality of identities; each one of us belongs to more than one aggregating dimension, not just in terms of ethnicity, nationality or religion, but even in terms of taste, culture, passions, interests...Italicity might be an advantage in the new world system that is taking form.... The glocalized world will be a mixture of communities, which will no longer aggregate on the basis of old territorial criteria of boarders that are decided by the State-Nation, but rather on connections that go beyond geographical limits. And in

> this, the Italic way of being is an advantage. (*Italic Lessons* 44)

Bassetti urged us to "think of Italicity as a new form of shared and pluralistic experiences" (14) that transcend the geo-political borders of Italy. Rome, England, and Spain changed once they attempted colonization of the world beyond their borders, and today traditional notions of the nation-state are failing in an age when commerce and cultures defy national borders in their creation of new transnational possibilities driven by business and socio-political collaborations.

In this new book, Bassetti turns his earlier thinking into action by calling on Italics of the world to make Italicity "a political subject," and in doing so, find ways to use Italic to replace Italian so that the full impact of the Italian influence on the world can be better understood. What he's getting at is that we need new ways of thinking if we are to design the future, ways that move in sync with the reality of global thinking and transnational interactions. In doing so, Bassetti shows us the danger of relying on national identities that lead to phrases such as "Let's Make America Great Again," and invites us to think more glocally by identifying with those who left nations, for whatever reasons, yet maintained a sense of how that nation shaped them so that we might all "Make the World Great Together."

The goal is to first recognize this in yourself, then in others from around the world. In this way, the power of Italic people, whom he numbers as over 250 million, can be stronger than the power of Italian passport bearers, and act independently and without the traditional constraints that national paranoia creates. In this way, artists, scholars, workers and managers of all the of all the Italian hybrid cultures in the world will come to recognize the strength of working together to make the world a better place through their culturally common senses of creativity and artisanal innovation.

Bassetti sees that the power of uniting business and education can lead to the kind of interaction that is future oriented with the aims of turning us away from nations battling each other and towards nations working for the common good of all humans. In this way Bassetti's ideas coincide with new developments in Italian American Studies such as the establishment of the Italian Diaspora Studies Summer Seminar under the aegis of the John D. Calandra Italian American Institute/Queens College and the University of Calabria, that has moved Italian/American Studies into the 21st century by establishing new ways of organizing and studying the impact that Italian immigrants have had, not just in the United States of America (the focus of what has been traditionally referred to as Italian/American studies), but throughout the world where Italian immigrants have set up homes in new lands. This work is echoed by the recent success of the "Trans-

national Italies" exhibition project, led by Dr. Lore-
dana Polezzi of the University of Cardiff and Dr.
Charles F. Burnett of the University of Bristol, who
have made the Italian Diaspora experience from
many countries speak to today's viewer in both
space and time, globalizing the notion of Italian
heritage so that it speaks not only to, but also beyond, national borders.

In light of these and many other developments,
Bassetti wants us to turn the provincial "Made in
Italy" into "Made by Italics" and see the "brain
drain" of Italian youth, as positive possibilities for
developing the idea of a global Italian becoming the
Italic who will serve humanity before nation for the
good of the world.

Bassetti's thinking makes the Italic possible, and
this manifesto makes it probable.

WORK CITED

Bassetti, Piero and Niccolò D'Aquino, eds. *Italic Lessons*.
Gail McDowell, trans. New York: Bordighera Press,
2010.

Fischer, Michael J. "Ethnicity and the Post-Modern Arts
of Memory." *Writing Culture: The Poetics and Politics
of Ethnography*. Eds. James Clifford and George E.
Marcus. Berkeley: U of California P, 1986. 194-233.

Let's Wake Up, Italics!

INTRODUCTION

A wake-up call, a rallying cry. This is the genesis of these pages; they are an appeal to people all over the world who are willing to listen. It is a message aimed at the millions of people I will call "Italics" in this book. Women and men who will read this book and, I hope, become aware of the potential reality of a global community and of the possibility of making it a topic of world history.

This is, without a doubt, an ambitious objective. It did not arise from nothing, but rather is another step in the journey of an idea catalyzed by a series of personal experiences. Experiences that developed through my political role in the Lombardy Region and, above all, as the President of Assocamerestero — an association that brings together the Italian Chambers of Commerce throughout the world — and of Globus et Locus, an operational entity created to help our ruling classes respond to the challenges of the glocal world.

During the 1980s and '90s, my work with Assocamerestero revealed to me the existence of a business community whose aggregation revolved around a much broader concept than merely a national one, and whose potential was much more extensive. As well, thanks to Globus et Locus, I was able to broaden my vision toward the existence of aggregations that were much more comprehensive and complex than traditional citizenship and nationality.

Over the past twenty years of my cultural and political activity, I have been a first-hand witness to the radical changes proposed by globalization, from both an economic and a social standpoint.

This has led to the intuition I will propound in this book: the existence of a "fact," of a well-defined reality, the presence in the world of millions of people we must become accustomed to calling "Italics."

This definition has taken shape over time and, after overcoming inevitable resistance, it has become widely accepted.

In fact, Italics are not just Italian citizens in Italy and abroad. They are, above all, the people of Canton Ticino, Dalmatia, and San Marino, and their descendants; Italian Americans, those of the two Americas and of Australia; as well as Italian speakers and all those people who might not have a drop of Italian blood in their veins, but have nonetheless embraced our county's values, lifestyle, and shared behavioral models.

I estimate that we are talking about approximately 250 million people.

They have different citizenships; they live in countries and societies that are far apart, both culturally and geographically. They speak different languages. But they feel the same.

Italicity is this shared way of feeling, a way of relating to the world, of giving meaning to the world, and it could transform itself into an opportunity for Italics to play a new leading role in global history.

Today, proposing a similar vision is more imperative than ever, since it would permit an inversion that would give emigration a new meaning: From a diaspora, it would become the process that sets the basis for new systems of aggregation.

The world is rapidly becoming more glocal. Already today, but even more so in the near future, the difference will be made by the relationship between the global dimension of events and their concrete, local consequences. And this is the heart of my message: The Italic community can and must acknowledge its — achieved — status as a "civilization," in the sense of a world community that bears the indisputable values of universality, taste, sociality, and urbanism.

My wake-up call is for this community and its members; I urge them to become aware of their potential and to foster the aggregation of a global community, founded on shared values, interests, and experiences. An exhortation at the crossroads between a call to reality and a new vision of the future, between gaining consciousness of an ongoing situation and the awareness that the history of Italicity rests on solid foundations and distinct outlines and is already active and operative today. And it is now called on to definitively affirm its relevance as a global player.

Italicity, reticulated and with a network that is often virtual/digital, develops through the values that the members of this community conserve and develop. Day after day, they are able to perpetuate a community of shared feeling that has been disseminated over the centuries.

One point must be stressed: Recognizing oneself as a member of this community does not mean renouncing one's own identity or national membership. Rather, it is an invitation to surpass and strengthen them, by enhancing the reality that is ours through citizenship with a second membership that is even broader and more enriching.

Italics know that the world has changed. They form and belong to a glocal community that is called on to act as a "world" community; they construct their identity in societies that are increasingly liquid and mobile, on the perimeter of the glocal world, which is all-inclusive but also strongly localized. They do not fear losing their special character. In fact, the Italic identity is pluri-identitary and in no way obliges them to be either Italian or American, either Italian or French or Argentine. Since it is a world community, this membership can become broader and less defined, but also, for this very reason, richer.

There are other, similar examples in the world: the English nation gave rise to the Anglo-Saxon community; Spain generated the Hispanic communitas, and Portugal, the Lusitanian ones. And now, from Italy, we have the Italic community.

In other words, there is a value-based and cultural presence in the world that transcends the Italian national dimension. And I have often encountered it in my experience as a political organizer.

In order to foster this process, Italics throughout the world must be urged to make full use of the values and practices of their civilization, to make more history together. This means helping them realize that there are many, many more of them than the 60 million Italians living in Italy. They need to be spurred to create something that can become a reality only within a context of widespread collaboration. And they must be put at the foundation of a new, original political subject that can collaborate in constructing the planet's new glocal order.

Communities like the Anglo-Saxon or Hispanic ones, that revitalize different realities such as the Commonwealth and the Hispanidad, have already partially marked the path to follow, redesigning it on the basis of their functional economic relations and adapting it, within a new global logic, to the predisposed relations through their historical and political affairs.

By gaining inspiration from these models, we will see how we Italics can also help give new stimulus and vitality to our presence in the world. Naturally, without presuming to offer definitive historical interpretations or identify clear-cut and incontrovertible forms of states. This would be contrary to the very nature of the dynamics described here.

Thus, in the following pages, the aim is to put into effect the sense of a vision, to outline the possible pathway that can reveal it, to encourage the emergence of an awareness that, I hope, will become a common feeling. Well-grounded experience, theoretic elaborations matured through encounters with great thinkers and through field research: ideas that aim at understanding and fostering the process of aggregation, identifying what bonds Italics together and what can lead them to form this transnational polis.

It is no coincidence that business is the starting point — not only because I began these reflections in afferent places (Chambers of Commerce), but because these values and interests are incarnated primarily in business. And from this initial terrain, through the organization of civil society and the development of a ruling class, we can arrive at the topic of politics, or rather, the ability to influence the decision-making process within its new glocal dimension.

In virtue of the fluidity and evolvement of the processes described, I hope that Italics — to whom these elaborations and reflections are addressed — will enrich this reading, establishing with it that fruitful relationship proper to "open texts."

It is an invitation to those who decide to become part of this community: to animate it, to enrich it, through a voluntary and multiform adhesion that invests our very identity, in this world that is increasingly basted and sewn by global and glocal dynamics.

1.

THE WORLD IS CHANGING

How It All Began

The year was 1993. I had recently been elected president of Assocamerestero and was working with a number of collaborators to increase the relevance of Italy's Chambers of Commerce abroad.[1]

Our attention was directed not only at how they functioned, but also at understanding their true nature. A few points were clear: For example, the Chambers of Commerce were not merely alliances of businesspeople; in virtue of their associative character, they were dedicated to encouraging the growth of relationships — economic, cultural, and social — among their members; they had long ago ceased be-

---

[1] Basically, Chambers of Commerce are aggregators which serve, generate, and oversee business communities. For example, the Italian Chamber of Commerce in New York represents a mixed Italian American business community, composed of Italians with interests in the United States and Americans with interests in Italy. Obviously, the community is patronized by Americans, Italians, and Italian-Americans, i.e., by people who live in the United States and have Italian roots, but also by "true-blue" Americans who are interested in doing business with Italy. An initial difference emerged after frequenting the "official" Italy of diplomatic circles within the framework of my Assocamerestero activities: "Italian" Italy wanted, above all, to affirm Italianism, for example by trying to convince Americans of Italian origin to apply for an Italian passport. Instead, the business community behaved in a substantially stateless manner: Rather than sharing national values per se, it felt it shared attitudes, tastes, and mentality.

9

ing only a "window" for business dealings with Italy. Only rarely did they limit themselves to affirming the Italianism of their business in the area where they were active; more often, they interpreted the many needs of a business population that was one-third Italian, one-third local, and one-third mixed. In other words, they operated within a three-dimensional logic: a multiform reality, which was neither Italian nor local, but rather a third category.

In the Chambers of Commerce abroad, the so-called mixed businesses weren't searching for a common ground with Italian businesses; on the contrary, their aim was to find possibilities for collaboration that revolved around recognition of their own identity, of which their Italian identity was only a component, albeit an important one. This was true in every Chamber of Commerce abroad, in Argentina as in the United States or Australia.

That is when I realized that the shared character that permitted the Chambers of Commerce abroad to create their own system wasn't strictly Italianism, but rather a hybrid dimension, of which — as I mentioned — Italianism was merely one of the founding factors. Two other factors were almost always present: One was the effectively local element; the other, that the entrepreneurs (with full citizenship and local political loyalty) did not disdain, but rather aspired to be considered hybridized with the world in which they did business. But here, too, there were various facets: Many of these entrepreneurs had dual citizenship; others were firmly determined to glorify their local assimilation, which they had achieved with great effort.

This situation, which appeared legitimate when viewed as a catalyzing principle of the Chambers of Commerce's institutional — and thus political — affiliation, posed quite a few problems. The Chambers existed thanks to the support of the Italian state, and, to a certain degree, this bond implied loyalty to Italianism. The Chambers of Commerce were considered Italian by the Consuls and Ambassadors, foreign entrepreneurs, and the Minister of Commerce. But this did not fully dovetail with the convictions of two-thirds of the people who frequented them and who were not Italian. Naturally, these people, even if they did not hold an Italian passport, were often of Italian origin. But this did not imply an a priori or total identification with the political experience of the country which had in a certain sense "expelled" them. On the contrary. And so: If the nature of their so-called "colleagueship" wasn't Italianism, in the sense of citizenship, what tied it all together?

An episode made everything clear to me. In that period, the agricultural policy of the European Community had blocked the import of goods from countries like Argentina. The producers of Italian pasta needed more durum wheat than Europe could produce in order to satisfy the export needs of countries like the United States. A way had to be found to sidestep the obstacle of the limitation of imports set by the EU's Common Agricultural Policy (CAP). The Chambers of Commerce of Buenos Aires and New York began to talk with each other. I don't remember who came up with the idea, but after a few telephone calls a solution was found. Different entrepreneurs in four countries began to collaborate together in order to produce pasta in Costa Rica, using Argentine wheat, Italian knowhow and brands, and the marketing ability of a regular importer registered at New York's Italian Chamber of Commerce, an American of Italian origin, and as such well introduced in New York's Italian restaurants.

What had facilitated this solution?

Certainly not Italianism, because the initial entrepreneur was Costa Rican, and the importer was American. Perhaps a shared familiarity with the pasta business? Or a natural propensity for dialogue?

In other words: Would an operation like this have been possible without a cultural commonality or a shared way of doing business? I most definitely thought not. And in fact, I soon found that both the Costa Rican and the American, even though they did not have Italian citizenship, both had a specific style of doing business in which the Italian component, although not dominant, was strongly present.

The problem promised to be complex, and, stimulated by these reflections, I decided we needed to put ourselves in the hands of professionals with extensive experience in studying Italian migration. I commissioned the sociologists Consuelo Corradi and Enrico Pozzi to research the Italian American business community in the countries in question.

The outcome of their study confirmed my hypotheses. Their research showed that many of the Italian Chambers of Commerce in America interrelated with a "world" that was neither the world of Italy nor that of another country, but rather expressed something its members had in common. The prevalent logic was not only business-related. It was a special relationship that also involved other attitudes and feelings that ranged from patriotism to social commitment and style.

Furthermore, I noted that the system of cultural values of reference for the business community that frequented the Chambers of Commerce abroad went well beyond the international sphere because, in advance, it grasped problems that were clearly glocal.

But that wasn't all. Something else caught my attention: I noticed that the business people registered at the Chambers of Commerce were not aware of the common trait their business experiences shared. Thus, not even they knew what was influencing their way of interrelating, that heretofore unknown "extra something" which aggregated them

— as borne out by the research — both economically and socially. We needed to get to the bottom of this. Even at the risk of inevitable complexities.

We had to provide an answer regarding the nature of that third category, which was, and still is, the deciding factor of the entire mechanism.

The scholars realized this after studying the personal phone directories and appointment calendars of the people registered at the Chambers of Commerce who agreed to participate in the study. By observing their relational dynamics, Corradi and Pozzi noted complex overlaps between motivations of citizenship and those of commercial functionality, following empathies that related to more than just ethnic-cultural affinities.

Guaranteeing professional secrecy, the two researchers were given access to the agendas of those participating in the research project. Always ensuring the maximum discretion, they then requested and were given permission to follow the businesspeople in their activities for a week. Their suspicions were confirmed: The Italic entrepreneurs — even though they denied it, almost certainly in good faith — primarily dealt with, did business with, and dialogued with "those of their kind." When, at the end of the week of observation, this fact was brought to their attention, they were amazed.

In other words, they appreciated being part of the establishment of the country in which they lived and worked, but in practice they dealt primarily with ... other Italics.

But there was more. The undeniable preference for Italianism always went in tandem with concrete interests. This was obvious in what is known as the Italian-sounding phenomenon. Take, for example, the case of the Parmigiano Reggiano imitation that goes by the name of Parmesan: one of the many products made throughout the world — sometimes with questionable results — that are inspired by the values, the culture, and the traditions of products that are truly Made in Italy. It is clear that the aggregating element of that business was not the Italianism of the cheese but the fact that it sounded Italian. Back then, this created major problems — and it still does — on the level of primarily Italian commercial interests: The Italians were for the Parmigiano, but many more entrepreneurs among the Italics were interested in the Parmesan!

It became progressively clear that Italianism was not the equivalent of what only later would we call Italicity. For this reason, when it came time to choose the title for the research, we rejected "The World of Italians Abroad" and coined "The World in Italian", in an attempt to seize that extra something which still eluded us.

More in general, we were struck by two aspects:

> First, in the emerging glocal economic world, interpersonal relations were fueled by more

than just comparisons and exchanges between markets of different nationalities. The relational flows of the entrepreneurs increasingly crossed borders. The traditional national markets and their trans-border relations were being replaced by a large glocal market, whose needs were much better served by a network of mixed Chambers of Commerce rather than a sunburst of Italian Chambers of Commerce Abroad, arranged like rays around a single national center.

Second, the problem of the ongoing relations among Italian businesspeople abroad could neither be comprehended nor explained on the basis of the traditional hypothesis of the bilateral dialogue among people who were considered only according to their respective nationalities.

Naturally, this was a process in the making. But these changes were able to strongly influence the economic relations and the relationships not only among the Chambers of Commerce, but also among the relative business communities and among the cultural and social worlds these business communities had evoked.

It was obvious that even the national economic dimension was becoming nothing more than the tip of an iceberg submerged in the new cultural, existential, and thus social (and also potentially political) dimension of what we used to call the Italian-foreign community.

It was becoming increasingly clear to me that soon there would no longer exist places that were not crossed by global flows of various types, nor would there be global flows that were not parsed according to the characteristics of these places. Words like "glocalization" and "glocalism" would become the new lenses through which reality would be read.

I determined that this process needed to be identified and we needed to gain awareness of it: The international world was waning and was giving way to the glocal world.

Encountering The Glocal Dimension

But after all, there was no way I could not know. I was reminded every day by my new responsibilities. After leaving the presidency of Associamerestero in 1999, I founded the association Globus et Locus. As a result, my reflections on the phenomenon of glocalization shifted to this new structure created by the convergence of the world of the Chambers of Commerce (universitas mercatorum) and the academic world (universitas studiorum), more specifically, the Catholic University of the Sacred Heart, which was chosen for its potentially universalistic vocation.[2] Slowly but surely, and in different forms, Regions, Municipalities, Chambers of Commerce, and banking foundations joined Globus et Locus. The association's mission is to help the managerial class face the challenges of glocalization by providing them with a new politi-

---

[2] For a description of the history and activities of Globus et Locus' Italics project, please refer to this book's Appendix.

cal culture and a system of updated values which have adopted glocalism (i.e., those phenomena that derive from the impact of globalization with local realities, and vice versa) as the key for interpreting reality. An extremely intriguing task. It was already highlighting the dialectics destined to leave a mark on our era and, through profound changes, influence the lives of people, economies, societies, and institutions.

It immediately became clear that this would not be an easy task. I realized this when it came time to choose the association's name and logo.

I opted for Latin in order to achieve the precise semantics, which the originality of the topics demanded. In Italian, *luogo* (place) refers to the territory and putting down roots; the Latin word locus refers to a sort of clearing or glade, a space that is formed in relation to what surrounds it, regardless of what it contains. It is not simply a piece of a territory. It is a nexus of functions and services. Therefore, what better word than locus to describe the glocal dimension, which champions functional institutions over traditional ones?

The association's logo was even more difficult to define. We needed to condense into one graphic symbol the intentions of what was already a pioneering creation. Which image representing the entire globe could depict the challenge that had spurred us to investigate the new dimensions of how we exist, work, perceive others, and react?

Italo Lupi, a friend and well-known architect, synthesized the essence of our challenge in a few pen strokes. The result of his work is the image on the book's cover: a black circle — the globe — that contains within itself another smaller circle, contrasting but encompassed. And next to it, outside the larger black circle, a third circle with the qualities of the preceding two: black, like the first, but the same size as the second, smaller one.

Glocalization in a nutshell. A dimension in which the local is outside the global; it distances itself in its quality and spatial position but at the same time is an intimate and vital component, fundamental in configuring the whole, but without being reduced to a mere addition that completes it. An image which calls to mind a ballet of meanings, provenances, declensions. A dialectic between the universal and the particular, each of which is able to contain the other and refer to it, with different paths and in constant evolution.

From a symbolic point of view, Lupi's design was a highly efficient synthesis. Using the language of artistic intuition, it helped us understand the processes through which the world order was being irremediably surpassed (and replaced by a different one).

The revolution caused by technological innovation, which was initially called globalization, and later, glocalization, revealed itself in its true light: an epochal turning point.

By nullifying space and time, it catalyzed a change in the organizational paradigms of the world and of society. Its breadth and scope can only be compared to the great changes that have occurred in the history of mankind, such as the agricultural revolution, which transformed the human condition when people developed procedures that allowed them to put down roots. Instead, today, humanity is experimenting with the opposite phenomenon, the discovery that it is possible to live in a context dominated by the mobility of people, things, and signs.

This revolution could not help but affect the values underpinning human coexistence, such as nationality, so close to our heart. If the act of putting down roots, which generated nations, entails a preference for everything that evokes division (borders, distinctions, separations, strict citizenships, mono-identity), mobility tends to promote encounter, assimilation, pluri-citizenship, pluri-identities, and thus the value of hybridization. One of the first problems glocalism encountered was, in fact, the relationship between global and local and, on the cultural and social level, how to reconcile individualization and hybridization, in light of the dimension of pluri-identities we are all immersed in.

Naturally, it was already clear that the metaphor of "roots" and the successive "uprooting" was by now obsolete, and Zygmunt Bauman's suggestion seemed more in keeping with the times, when he wrote: "Unlike 'uprooting' and 'disembedding,' there is nothing irrevocable, let alone ultimate, in weighing anchor. While roots torn out of the soil in which they were growing are likely to desiccate and die, anchors are drawn up only to be dropped again elsewhere, and they can be dropped with similar ease at many different and distant ports of call" (Bauman, 2009).

Even more concretely: The turning point also meant abandoning the idea of auctoritas — authority — which had been, and still is, dominant in national states; in other words, the monopoly of legitimate violence as an instrument to guarantee sovereignty and control over one's own territory.

By changing the values and lifestyles, it was easy to imagine that institutional and political orders, too, would be forced to make adaptations that were difficult to configure.

We were thus faced with a watershed situation.

Until yesterday, the organization of the modern world, conceived and projected on the assumption of the value of putting down roots, had identified the state (and not by chance) as a political subject constituted by mankind to be a factor of security and stability. This is revealed by the very word 'state'. In Latin, the word 'status', from which the Italian 'stato' and the English 'state' derive, is the past participle of the verb 'stare', which in English can mean to 'stay put'. Thus, as Alberto Savinio notes, in Italian "the state reveals itself in its very name. Stato, before being the state, is 'stato,' the past participle of 'stare,' a verb which means to cease movement, to stop, to remain." With the advent of globalization, which on the contrary was devised on the assumption of mobility, new forms of statehood, citizenship, and assimilation were coming to the fore. The challenge was to update the traditional identitary categories — cultural, social, and political — within the framework of the new emerging institutions. The idea of the nation-state was in crisis. The institutional mechanisms were losing their power and their role, not only bottom-up (continentalism, glocalism), but top-down as well, toward the new "local." New, emerging political geographies were subverting the ties between national spaces and subnational or meta-national spaces (take, for example, Scotland and Catalonia, but also Brexit's impact on Europe). Cases such as the Laplanders' emerged where, in the presence of a cultural-political identity that did not correspond to a national state, effective solutions had already been found to achieve their recognition.[3]

Instead of our debates on *ius solis* ("right of the soil") and *ius sanguinis* ("right of blood"), the question of a progressive redefinition of identity and membership was coming to the fore; the need for a

---

[3] The governments of Norway, Sweden, and Finland long ago pinpointed a combination of objective and subjective criteria that would permit the Laplanders, as such (and not only as citizens of their respective national states), to vote. In order to do so, every adult Laplander must: a) declare he or she feels Lappish; b) regularly speaks in the Lapp language or has a parent or grandparent who can.

debate on the growing political presence of metropolitan cities was affirming itself. Global cities, in the words of Saskia Sassen, began to be recognized as "strategic sites for the management of the global economy and the production of the most advanced services and financial operations that have become key inputs for that work of managing economic operations."

Proof of this can be had by considering the case of the citizens of any of the member states of the European Union. These people are already no longer only Italian, French, or Spanish; rather, besides being Italian, French, or Spanish, they are also European. At the same time, these very same citizens — if Scottish, Catalonian, Belgian, Francophone, Padanian — also want to define themselves in light of this territorial membership. It was time to understand how the emerging political geographies inevitably overturned not only the morphology of the migratory phenomena, but their substance as well. To comprehend the truth of this affirmation, just consider the difference between a contemporary protagonist of the so-called "human capital flight" and a proletarian migrant of the early 1900s.

The space in which today's relations, interests, and exchanges intertwine is, thus, a global territory, whereas coexistence and membership are oriented toward the local. The two dimensions can cohabit only if they realize they are intertwined by new modalities: those of glocalism.

Beyond The Borders: Ideas In Evolution

We were presented with a new context. It was becoming increasingly clear that individual and collective identities were profoundly changing: Glocalization was introducing new communities and institutions into political history, powers that not only were formed top-down, but also that manifested themselves in bottom-up aggregations. Even in politics, open-source processes (part and parcel of those already present on the Web) configured new schema of community or functional aggregations built around institutional and political structures that differed from those based on territory. New methods of cultural, social, economic, and political aggregation were asserting themselves. If moving no longer necessarily means migrating, then even a passport no longer means citizenship, and territory no longer has to be synonymous with identity. And even in the antinomy between *ius soli* and *ius sanguinis*, recovering the value of hybridity meant substituting a concept of fixedness (the sŏliu[m] was the seat, the throne which guaranteed the right of blood in royal lineage) with one of fluidity, or rather, of mobility.

A new world was arising in which people could no longer assert that their identity was defined by a history or a culture of national membership. In this new world, people can live their own identity differently, depending on the degree to which they consider themselves hybridized with their context of residence: An Italian American in Little Italy lives and feels differently from an Italian American in San Francisco.

I could observe all this in tangible facts.

In the business communities in which I interwove relations, it was becoming increasingly clear that the taboo dividing people who lived and did business together by nationality was waning; it was becoming the norm to hold two passports — one of origin and one of residence. But in my opinion, the most interesting fact was that many of us were finding we could live and do business better by using more than one identity or by using a hybrid national identity.

I came from the world of politics — local and national — and to me, this situation was intriguing, to say the least.

On the horizon, a difficult path of reflections came into view.

I decided to follow that path.

During this phase, I came into contact with the thinking, and the effective collaboration, of two exceptional people, Amartya Sen and Zygmunt Bauman, and my discussions with them were augmented by a series of ideas that were being progressively generated by the world of the Chambers of Commerce.

In 2004, during a seminar in Turin promoted by Globus et Locus on the topic of glocalization and its impact on U.N. governance, I discussed with Sen the difficulties we were encountering in our research on a new identitary and socio-political categorization. Well, not only did he encourage us to continue our reflections on the topic, but he invited us to cross-correlate them with the concept of pluri-identities he was studying at the time. *In Identity and Violence*, he urged that we recognize the fact that there are many identities in the globalized world, and that today anyone can be connoted and enriched by a series of pluri-memberships, as long as he or she accepts them as their own.

"Of course," writes Sen, "we do know in fact that any real human being belongs to many different groups, through birth, associations and alliances. Each of these group identities can — and sometimes does — give the person a sense of affiliation and loyalty. Despite this, the assumption of singular affiliation is amazingly popular, if only implicitly, among several groups of social theorists. [...] The intricacies of plural groups and multiple loyalties are obliterated by seeing each person as firmly embedded in exactly one affiliation, replacing the richness of leading an abundant human life with the formulaic narrowness of insisting that any person is 'situated' in just one organic pack."

To Sen, in our glocal world, identity is increasingly less a given and increasingly more a process in evolution. It is a constant development which elects local territories as its theatre of action, where communities of various diasporas coexist and interweave. But it is also the virtual-global place of various networks, where encounters between people and signs can foster the creation of new groups of people within a worldwide context. A place where it is normal to belong to a community that is no longer monolithic, not just ethnic, linguistic, or institutional, but rather cultural and value-based. A community that is chosen, rather than imposed by a passport; where the concepts of citizenship and nationality are ebbing.

The only necessary prerequisite: to find one's place in this new world, so different from the world dominated by the traditional inter-national order and regulated by rigid borders.

The challenge, thus, is all-encompassing. Not just political, but involving ideas and civilizations as well. All this in a world in which innovative technologies are ceaselessly creating new opportunities for encounters or divergences.

For his part, Zygmunt Bauman helped clarify a point that was no less important: the possibility that people of different origins and with different dispositions and interests could meet and coexist in functionally compact communities without generating friction or intolerance. In fact, Bauman began an article on immigration and identity in the globalized world with the discovery made two years

earlier by a group of researchers from the Zoologi-
cal Society of London who went to Panama to
study the behavior of wasps, highly social insects.

For over six thousand hours, the London researchers monitored the movements of four hundred twenty-two wasps belonging to thirty three
different nests, and made an interesting discovery:
During their observation period, 56% of the monitored insects changed nests. Over half of them. As
though they had a passport or a visa, the Panamanian wasps had transferred from one nest to another, from one society to another. They had done so
"legitimately," without the new community calling
their membership or admittance into question. In
the new territories, they conducted their regular life
and carried out their duties, procuring food and
sharing it, with the other wasps. Not like tempo-
rary guests, but like new members of their recently-
adopted society, by no means opposed or rejected,
but rather integrated into the social life of this second community.

It was a true overturning of what official science had believed about the social life of insects:
that their "sociability" was confined to their community of membership. This interpretation took for
granted that a "state of nature" existed in which
each colony corresponded to a population that was
"legitimate," domiciled, originally from that place,
and impermeable to the arrival of "foreign" insects,
which would have been rejected as invaders be-

cause potentially able to compromise the colony's equilibrium. Exactly what we hear repeated today in certain populist speeches...

But — and this is the crucial point of Bauman's argument — even this discovery was the result of a change that was opening our eyes to the projection of human desires and fears in the theorization of closed societies. In fact, the researchers who had studied the Panamanian wasps belonged to a generation to whom multiculturalism was "natural."

The 33 wasp nests studied by the London researchers represent open societies, able to spontaneously re-balance potential imbalances, caused when a number of members abandon the nest, by harmoniously absorbing new arrivals. And all this without a "command center" to direct the traffic. Because the coming and going from one colony to another ensures the propagation of knowhow in all the wasp nests.

In other words, to Bauman, the various cognitive maps of the researchers of the old and the new generations simply reflect the passage from one phase of human history (during which nations were constructed) to a new multicultural phase. Bauman holds that, today, almost every country is populated by a multiplicity of diasporas, marked by the double process of immigration and emigration, of leaving and arriving. Thus, the global (and glocal) researcher/citizen is presented with a different state of nature from what is currently theorized in certain political circles, but that is equally "natural," since nowadays we are all like the Panamanian wasps, to a greater or lesser degree.

In synthesis, Bauman only reminded us that Nature already knows what mankind is now experiencing through the effects of mobility and glocalization: a new relationship between oneself, one's own territory, and one's own community; between oneself and the political-cultural circles of values and interests affecting the private, individual, employment, and social spheres.

A New Aggregating Factor

I found these analyses very important. They highlighted a glocal "state of nature" that was new and certainly quite up-to-date. They explained to me why today's national territories and their economies can be considered not just completed patchworks but junctions of networks, homelands of departures and arrivals for migrated or migrating populations, public spaces in which one's own identity can be renegotiated, places to direct the flows that can rebalance the excess or scarcity of resources, and in which competences can be transmitted through the mobility of their members. In turn, by moving, these members generate new "crossbreeds," kinships, hybrid communities in each of the national realities which are economically and politically affected. Above all, these analyses, by not limiting themselves to the sole reality of business but by extending their results to the entire glocal society, shed new light on what had still seemed enigmatic to me in my experience with Assocamerestero: how and why the system of Chambers of Commerce abroad could be more than just a place for comparison and encounter between various national business communities, and instead could reveal themselves to be a true "world." That World in Italian we had identified in 1995, albeit without finding a new definition for it.

The truth was that, first of all, it was a world inhabited by Italians and non-Italians registered with the Chambers of Commerce, whose culture and interests were to varying degrees hybridized with Italian business. But, through social and cultural connections, this world also extended to the local society in which the Italian Chambers of Commerce abroad had their branches, and, thus, it embraced not only the businesspeople but also the many consumers and clients who, in various ways, participated in the system of interests of the business community in question.

Secondly, this world also included aggregating factors that differed from those provided by international relations among the bearers of different passports and it was able to add new common factors that could be attributed to the aspects of hybridization generated by the various local encounters at each Chamber of Commerce. These common factors were in addition to the paradigms of the system that had been formulated in modern times with the national states, in which they did not seem able to bear citizenship but in which they undoubtedly proved to be something extra: almost an aggregator of the glocal dimension.

This was the specific aggregator of the world that was appearing before my eyes. An aggregator that needed to be further identified and cultivated in depth.

2.

ITALICITY

The Importance of A Name

Thus, we had to try to provide answers to what had become pressing questions.

What were the characteristics, the virtues, the objectives, the political structure of this "new world"? And what was the best term to define it?

I began with this latter question.

I started with the assumption that Italics represent more than the small reality of the business communities of approximately fifty Italian Chambers of Commerce abroad, which we had called a World in Italian. We had to find a name for this world.

This phrase no longer sufficed to express the intricate combination of interests, bonds of affinities, and cultures that we were learning more about with the passing years. I realized that World in Italian could describe neither the exact dimensions nor the true essence of the reality we wanted to represent: a reality that was, in fact, bigger and had a different identity. It was bigger because it went beyond the mere system of interests of a group of businesses and extended itself to the community of people —

primarily consumers — who had dealings with that system. It had a different identity because it included a network of communities of entrepreneurs and consumers who could not be strictly defined as Italian, since generally they were composed of a small percentage of Italians and a majority of people who were not Italian (at least not in the strict sense of Italian citizenship).

The adjective "Italic" seemed a much better fit to me.

This choice was only apparently lexical, and, significantly, early on it was not easy to accept this term among the many we considered. In part because lots of people — and with a certain degree of reason — considered the adjectives "Italian" and "Italic" equivalent. In part because introducing a new and spurious distinction raised suspicions of declassification in those who, if their hybridization were pointed out to them, could have felt relegated to a position of inferiority compared to those who were classified as ("pure") Italians. Not least because even historical studies seem to have canceled the past of the ancient populations to which the term *Italic* is rightly applied.

I decided to concentrate my attention on this problem.

Globus et Locus: Thoughts And Action

It was not an easy process. It took a lot of work, but today I think I can safely say that the term *Italics* has been accepted.

Our efforts revolved around our decision to base this recognition on politics and not on terminology. In the certainty that sociological categories are not eternal and must be redefined — just as identities must be renegotiated, as we have seen. Because, if problems arise from norms, then solutions can only arise from the synthesis of norms and updated thought (which keeps pace with the reality we live in).

In 2001, one of our first initiatives to this end was our participation in organizing the first Convention of Italians in the World, which was held with the patronage of the Ministry of Foreign Affairs. It was followed by the event "Notes for a schedule of meetings with various Italian communities in Australia." We then organized a series of international conferences in collaboration with CUA, the Catholic University of America, and with the Università Cattolica del Sacro Cuore of Milan. During the meetings in this authoritative international context, and upon the urging of the Italian American communities of Washington D.C. and New York, for the first time we proposed in an organic way our innovative elaboration on the topic of Italics.

Thanks to the interest that progressively grew in various parts of the world, the concept of Italicity found a broader terrain of consolidation. Globus et Locus was promoted and participated at numerous initiatives involving scientific, academic, media, business, and language communities; our association also collaborated with television and radio, universities, newspapers, journals, etc.

In particular, these most recent years have marked an important step forward in the perception of Italicity as a historical "fact." One of the major and most innovative political-cultural contributions was provided by the University of Pennsylvania. In 2011, a number of conferences and flourishing editorial activity led to a series of publications in which Italicity was officially recognized, both linguistically and as a category.

One of the important conceptual passages was that from migration to new mobility; this transition was made possible by our work with the "Altreitalie" Center, which the Agnelli Foundation decided to transfer to Globus et Locus.

The data we have gathered over the years indicates that awareness of the complexity and originality of the "Italics phenomenon" has substantially changed. We have made an important observation in our delineation of the future scenario: Italics are beginning a process of aggregation around the substratum of values that will hasten the decline of the state-nation, surpassed by glocalization. Contrary to what has prevalently occurred in the past, this is coming about bottom-up.

All this is beginning to bear fruit. Recently, even institutional and diplomatic circles are apparently becoming aware of the importance of constructing a new paradigm, more complex and problematic than the traditional concept of the nation-state with its ongoing dynamics: a paradigm which accommodates concepts such as transnationalism, pluri-identities, hybridization, and Italicity.

A Story That Began Long Ago

A number of young historians helped put the question in focus. Their contribution proved to be fundamental because it showed me that only by going back to the pre-Roman populations (which historians unequivocally define as Italics) could we get to the heart of a problem which, although over two thousand years old, was in a certain sense regaining relevance in this new climate that was transcending cultures blocked in national schemas.

Where did the Italics come from? Is it possible to identify them only in recent times as the bearers of a contrived denomination, or should their presence be traced back to the era of the ancient populations which appeared under this name?

I have no doubt that the proper affirmation is the latter one, but how to explain to the multitudes that it is one thing to talk about Italics in the particular sense we want to give the term here; but it is quite another to talk about Italics but still refer to Italians, in substance.

Although current usage considers both terms substantially interchangeable, if we shift the discourse to the historical level, the events involving those people we call Italics prove to be something quite different from the people who today are defined politically as Italian. In fact, there is only a partial and chronologically limited overlap between Italic history and, in the strictest sense, Italian history. The times, the territories, the protagonists, the social forms, and the political structures are all different.

Whereas Italic history began in pre-Roman times, Italian political and state history had a shaky beginning in the Napoleonic era and gained its definitive structure only with the Risorgimento.

If Italian history is entirely contained within the schema of Westphalia (immersed in the topics of borders and nations-state that became dominant starting with the Peace of Westphalia in 1648), Italic history, on the contrary, has roots that go deep into antiquity and began in the perspective of spaces that were not yet delineated by territorial borders. In fact, with the possible exception of the Roman Empire, it developed outside of, or by means of, the various political organizations with which it came into contact, in a vision that was willing to mix with the various "globalities" that were progressively emerging in the world and that were constantly

challenging it, through different socio-political structures such as tribes, cities, empires, churches, ma-
neuvering localisms, and universalisms. Italic history was forged by the peculiar coexistence of an
undeniable anthropological-cultural unity and an
intricate fabric of hybridizations in the alternating
succession of political realities it faced: the Rome of
antiquity, the Vatican, the Holy Roman Empire, the
Renaissance, and the tardy recourse to the idea of a
national state. Italic dispersion has always had to
cope with environments with which it was forced
to hybridize without prevailing. Only Rome, perhaps because it was a master of hybridization, also
managed to prevail.

Thus, it was becoming increasingly clear that the
Italic path had started long ago. Historians tell us
that although its preparatory phase had been important for the Italian Peninsula, it had immediately projected itself outward: From the Romans to the
Genoese, the Venetians, the Florentines, the Lombards, etc., all the different and many regional and
local identities which make up the Italian peninsula
have traveled the seas and roads of the world, almost always integrated with currents of a global
nature (empire, religion, preaching, exploration, finance, diplomacy, art).

Along their pathways, and already at the beginning of the second millennium, colonies of merchants hailing from the Italian peninsula would
meet in London, Constantinople, Antwerp, Seville,

or Aleppo. In 1271, the Venetian Marco Polo, at only seventeen years of age, accompanied his father Niccolò and his uncle Matteo on his famous journey to the Far East that lasted twenty-four years. But Italic merchants and financiers were legion and active everywhere.

In 1283, Lombard Street in London had fourteen banks from Lombardy; in Paris, in 1292, there were twenty of them on Rue des Lombards. Not only merchants and financiers, but artists, teachers, architects, artisans, men of the church, and political exiles all navigated the pre-Columbus world.

The discovery of America and the birth of the New World generated other horizons for Italicity, which gradually extended its reach. Navigators and merchants, monks and priests, artists and intellectuals began to cross not just Europe, Asia, and Africa, but the Americas as well. Although the emigration of foreigners to the Americas was prohibited under Spanish dominion, between 1535 and 1538 the New World already counted six people originally from the Kingdom of Naples, two from the state of Milan, three from the Kingdom of Sicily, one from Lucca, one from Florence, fourteen from Genoa, one from Turin, one from Piedmont, and one from Cremona. In 1861, the year Italy was unified, many regional representatives of that diaspora — people from Piedmont, Lombardy, Veneto, Tuscany, Sicily, and so on — were already settled in every corner of the world.

This path was inspired by a thirst for knowledge, the Catholic faith, the dealings and interests of merchants, money and finance, diplomatic flair and finesse, art and research. It left a clear mark throughout the world: in the laws and the strategic organization in Roman times; in Catholic universalism after the decline of the classical era; in the philosophical or poetic communities during the Middle Ages; in the explorations and the aristocratic courts of the Renaissance, in the national states of modern times. But what prevailed were often factors such as humanistic sensitivity, a sense of beauty, a vocation for exploration, the genius of military command, diplomatic and administrative skill, and — above all in modern times — scientific genius, the innovative ability of single individuals, entrepreneurial ability.

In these circles, the Italic was almost always perceived as an influential person or member of vast networks and global aggregations, almost never as a participant in a self-declared political-state identity.

Only at this point did the drive toward nationalism begin: with the Unification of Italy, this diaspora became aware of being Italian, a "national" quality which began to interact with the various regional memberships. This objective appeared only with the Risorgimento, when the peninsular Italics — plus others from Ticino and San Marino — gave themselves the political goal of a national-state aggregation, which today is already waiting to be refashioned.

Italians And Italics: A Possible Overlap

But another question came to the fore: To what point, and in which terms, can the Italic and the Italian experiences be considered converging during the phase that lasted from the Risorgimento to World War II — historically and politically overlapping, but nonetheless diverse?

Italic history is millenary, of global inspiration and references; Italian history is shorter and coupled to the history of a specific territory: that portion of the Mediterranean peninsula which is geographically denominated Italian. The first was inspired by mobility, dispersion, hybridization. The second was constructed around ideals of nationalism, territorial stability, state power. The first was willing to participate in various ways in the history of other, politically quite diverse communities, wherever they were located — such as the China of Marco Polo or the Americas of Columbus and Vespucci. The second was forced to make clear-cut choices regarding its social and territorial position, that was often not self-determined: sovereign in Italy, excluding Ticino and San Marino; managerial class in Latin America; subordinate in North America; working class in France, Germany, and Australia.

This diversity of circumstances was reflected in the diversity of the results. On a human and social level, the Italic experience had produced vast hybridizations. In Latin America these were fostered by similar social extractions; in North America by the melting pot (which combines all the particularities that new arrivals are called upon to put at the disposal of the community); in Australia by British customs. On the other hand, hybridization was hindered by national cohesion in France and Germany, for example. Only the hybridization of Italy, Ticino, and San Marino involved policies centered on efforts aimed at putting down roots, territorial separateness, national purity, short-lived colonialism.

This has been the contribution of history, and its ability to let us comprehend a pathway — Italicity's — which sprang forth as unitary, expanded greatly in the Mediterranean region during Roman times, consolidated itself in the Middle Ages, became multifarious yet still universalist during the Renaissance, partially diverged from the Italian pathway during its "nationalist" phase, and today, under the thrust of processes of glocalization, is on its way toward a renewed potential convergence.

This comprehension is no doubt valuable. But it must be integrated with many other facets if it is to respond to the further need to achieve greater awareness of the complex reality of Italics, to better evaluate the concrete possibilities of bringing together and integrating the two realities in question (Italic and Italian). And to get a clearer idea of how the Italics' vast anthropological, cultural, and social dimension — their quantitative dimension still needed to be estimated — can face history in a unitary way on the historical-cultural level, as well as on the other levels that are more fundamental than ever in the economic and political world.

I began with the problem of definitions and numbers.

All of us know who the Italians are and how many of them there are today: the X number of people holding an Italian passport in Italy, plus the Y number of them abroad.

But what about the Italics?

In order to count them we needed to first define them. We tried to do so. It wasn't easy, but in the end, we agreed upon the following definition (by now adopted and acquired).

A person attains Italicity when the culture of an individual of Italian origin or identification comes into contact with a different or distinct local culture and hybridizes with it. The person involved in this process will come into possession of cultural elements produced by the synthesis of the entire range of hybridizations. This basis (imbued with peninsular Italianism but also dissimilar because it is integrated with the multitude of cultures it has encountered) is Italicity, "something" whose power of attraction is enough to unite its possessors around a partial but analogous system of values, customs, and interests.

So then, what is Italicity?

It is a socio-cultural dimension which, in order to be embodied by the vast number of people described above, pinpoints an identity-making third category, which at the present time is pre-political, but is open to becoming political.

So then, who are today's Italics?

To answer with a quip and a list that is sure to impress, we could indicate the following peoples as Italics: Jorge Mario Bergoglio, Sergio Marchionne, Mario Balotelli, and Daniel Ricciardo. Or: Bill de Blasio, Nancy Pelosi, Elio Di Rupo, Leon Panetta, and more.

But to carry on this line of reasoning, we could go much further. If, in fact, the Italic presence in the world is the result of all the migratory phenomena and the mobility that have characterized our history, we could say that today's Italics are, above all, the citizens of the Italian Republic living in Italy (sixty million) and abroad (over four million); then there are the other inhabitants of the peninsula whose political organization differs from that of the Italian Republic: the Swiss in Canton Ticino (numbering over three hundred thousand residents in Ticino and roughly ten thousand abroad); the citizens of the Republic of San Marino (roughly three hundred thousand residents in the republic and a few thousand residing abroad); the Dalmatians and their fellow citizens abroad. To this we must add the tens of millions of people who have emigrated from Italy since its founding, as well the millions of their descendants who are to varying degrees "crossbreeds."

In this regard, the social sciences have created instruments that allow us to estimate the number of descendants from the various diasporas. For example, in the 1990s, the Agnelli Foundation had estimated there were fifty million Italian descendants in the world. According to other estimates (2013), today there are seventy million people of Italian extraction. To this must be added the descendants of people from Canton Ticino, San Marino, and Dalmatia.

Adding in the other Italian-speaking people who are neither Italian nor of Italian descent, the total approaches two hundred million.

And lastly, if one also includes those people who consider themselves true-blue Italics (or want to be considered such) through simple cultural affinity, the total rises to two hundred and fifty million people, and other estimates put them at even many more.

Naturally, this number is very imprecise. But after all, the founding characteristic of hybridization is that it has indistinct borders.

But just imagine the political significance of discovering there are so many more than just sixty million Italics.

It would mean belonging to something that, politically, is quite different. And I do not mean only in terms of quantity, but also, and above all, of identity.

To summarize: Over here, in the Italian Republic, we have a community which, despite the relative brevity of its unitary political experience, has tried to define itself around values such as territory, the clarity and value of its borders, blood relationships, political unity and sovereignty, and institutionalization of the state. Over there, in the universality of the world, we have a geographic dispersion made of potential mobility, hybridization, the laborious construction of new community relations, an absence of its own institutions.

In political terms: Over here, a state-national layout — and it is not difficult to foresee its involution under the growing pressure of glocalization. Over there, a growing state whose doors are being thrown open by a future hallmarked by a new type of political aggregation, that is still to be invented.

Are these two alternative prospects? No. They are two potentially converging prospects, to be aligned as the second prospect surpasses the first.

In fact, it is not a matter of counterposing the shorter path of Italianism (for now the only one that is familiar and cherished) within the historical pathway of Italicity.

The challenge is a different one: to configure the "new" organizational and political subject within which, in an aggregation of people far more numerous than those of the Italian peninsula, millions of Italics could find themselves facing their community and political future together, in a world that is no longer inter-national but glocal.

This challenge is already ongoing, as can be seen by the distress of national states tormented by the reorganization of their own regionalisms; by the difficulties of constructing Europe, hindered by a refusal to let the old national states flow into it and by the non-existence of any world assembly after the failed attempt to entrust it to a union of nations.

This is the challenge to which we want to wake Italics.

Wake them up to do what? To discover they are a diaspora? Or, rather, to elaborate a new institutional and political pathway that conforms to the particularities of the present-day world in which we have seen how the true founding category is, in fact, hybridization?

The third solution is the best. The one I would like to see take shape at the end of the process that will, I hope, be catalyzed by this wake-up call. A horizon in which millions of Italics discover they have been seized by the certainty of having found a new political container that is to Italicity what the national state had been to Italianism.

Embracing Hybridization

But for this to happen, we must first of all try to understand what effectively ties Italics together already today; because only in this way can we hope to give life to a unifying prospect, to something that is politically new.

It is worth repeating: The specificity of today's Italic community rests on its readiness to hybridize. As we have seen, this attitude is inherent in its system of values, and, through the centuries, it can be interpreted as the footprints left by the mobility of the Italian peninsula's inhabitants.

Obviously, the aggregating thrust of Italics does not come from here. Nor from feeling themselves part of a diaspora, as occurs in the Jewish tradition, which is constructed on its own religious credo. Naturally, the Italics also feel this powerful factor.

But if anything, what contemporary Italics feel is the need to maintain their special and distinctive propensity to embrace differences, something that has characterized them through the centuries and which they need to valorize today, throughout the world. Not just in Italy, but in all those territories where they have decided to live and hybridize themselves. A further challenge, for us Italians, in light of our relationship with the "new mobile population," or their descendants, the so-called G2 (the "second generations"), who have chosen to live in Italy.

In fact, it cannot be denied that in an interconnected world like ours today, we must rebuff the
demand to marginalize and reject migrants asking
for asylum. We cannot consider a return to a past of
separation, of borders.

Because it is just as clear that the concept of
immigration represents, in itself, a category that
has been rendered obsolete by the new emerging
concept of "mobility." We must learn to consider
the "new mobility" a true rejuvenation that is both
cultural and, in a certain sense, characteristic of societies that are wealthy but tired, developed but
unhappy, powerful but fragile.

3.

ITALICS: WHAT UNITES US

The general outlines of Italicity are becoming clear.

But what could we concretely do to fulfill its potential to the best degree possible?

How could we stimulate this worldwide community magma to compact itself to the point of achieving a specific historical subjectivity?

It is said that what traditionally unites people is sharing a territory, borders, frontiers. Today, glocalization, in part thanks to the impact of technology and the growing number of processes fostering mobility, has scaled back the importance of those factors.

As a result, a community of Italics, in order to be considered such, must aggregate itself in a different way, going beyond the nation-state paradigm.

This is dictated by the times we live in: We should free ourselves from the idea of belonging to a territory that is spatially defined, and forcefully bring new identitary reference points to the fore.

The future will be driven by hypotheses of political cohesion that cannot limit themselves to the usual nationalistic, ethnic-linguistic, juridical-institutional mechanisms. The winning factor will be the elaboration of proposals formulated within the perspective of a world community, and it will require efforts involving the anthropological, cultural, and functional spheres in order to be fully comprehended.

The new community will have neither dividing lines nor clear borders based on formal documents, such as passports or residency permits. It will have to proceed by steps that will refer to each individual person or group.

All this means that it will have to be constructed around binding factors that overlap with national references, without supplanting them. These binding factors will have to be based on organizational practices and on different symbolisms from those that will have been rendered obsolete. Identity will not spring from flags, hymns, or "military glories" — as per the "Westphalian" nationalistic logic that has characterized the modern era and produced such horrific wars.

The Italic dimension will be community-based and will take form around elements such as a shared history and values that will be sought in the perspective of a new logic.

It is something that all Italics are called to do. What is appearing before our eyes is, in fact, a true overturning of Massimo D'Azeglio's call to "make Italians." The Italics already exist!

The necessary step involves putting in focus the elements around which the idea of Italicity can coalesce. And this can only be done in a new way. By shelving the obsolete concepts of *ius soli* and *ius sanguinis* in favor of new contributions. For example, the *ius voluntatis* proposed by Michela Murgia: "I don't choose the land I am born in, or the blood of those who generated me, but I want a dimension of choice regarding my membership. I am the sum of many identities, but there is a dimension in which I can make a difference: my willpower. Who do I belong to? Which is my community of destiny, above and beyond that of land or blood? Can I decide to belong to that population, to belong to those collective destinies, instead of to those of my blood or of my land? What is the citizenship of the future based on?"

It is now clear that the topic of identity, historically the object of dramatic anguish, is returning forcefully to the fore. The starting point of this search of ours is emerging clearly: identitary reference points.

New Identities To Fulfill A Yearning For Homeland

Choosing to define oneself as Italic will mean welcoming a richer and multifaceted identity.

More precisely, the glocalist conviction, which we have decided to adopt as the interpretive key of our pathway, will accompany us on three levels: first, by initiating the necessary process to overcome the old national myths; second, by valorizing the idea of "miscegenation;" and finally, by validating the penchant for soft power rather than the violence of hard power in organizing the world.

Thus, in my opinion, an important cohesive factor for the Italic world community must be sought in the cognizant reference of Italics to their pluri-identity, in the construction of their specific "civil personality." It is not always easy, in fact, to accept that hybridization does not mean abandonment or, worse, "betrayal." To understand this point, all it takes is a reflection on the useless suffering forced on entire Italic communities during WWII, when they were suddenly forced to rediscover contrived political identities that were attributed to them. I refer to what happened in the United States when Italian Americans and Italian Germans were locked up in prisoner camps at the start of the Second World War. Or, consider what place the concept of "homeland" occupies in a globalized world dominated by the phenomenon of mobility. Over time, I have gone so far as to affirm that the need for a homeland can be conceived not as the conclusion of a process of unity, but as its catalyzing cause, as Petrarch teaches us.

If this is the case, Italics are called on to become aware of their shared patrimony of memories, values, languages, and way of feeling, and to make it their ideal homeland.

"To me, however, the whole world is a homeland, like the sea to fish," wrote Dante in *De vulgari eloquentia*. His perspective was neither municipalistic nor nationalistic. On the contrary, as we know, the Poet's verses and thoughts were driven by an ideal that was very modern and, to all effects, universalistic.

If the Risorgimento offered us the idea of "home" as a nation-state (with precise borders and sovereignty), today, in our search for the future in our past, the time has come to instead rediscover the political liquidity which has always characterized the Italic genus.

The "Open Source"

A second factor uniting Italics to be highlighted is the winning idea of modern socialization and communitarianism, which is so well synthesized by the concept of open sources. A founding pillar of the digital era is the conception of the network and digitalization as a historical opportunity for transparency and universal access to knowledge. This idea of the digital citizen fosters the liberation — even the political liberation — of the individual.

The concept of open sources overcomes the barriers of membership and offers itself to the interaction and contributions of anyone who wants to take part in writing code, in its evolution and improvement. It also means a radically different use of information and relations as an identifying instrument. And isn't this conglomeration of inventions, experiences, and tastes the basis of the aggregating phenomenon with which the traditional "Made in Italy" concept made its fortune, expanding itself into an "Italian way of life"?

A "thread linking Made in Italy and Italicity" has been discussed, and not by chance; in the words of the economist Stefano Micelli, "it is the open source nature of our cultural chromosomes that often makes our production, our savoir-faire interesting. Our products are so versatile that they rapidly become a natural component of the lifestyle and the daily life of other people." This process has developed by following dynamics of hybridization which have spontaneously resulted in various phenomena that enrich a presumed "original canon." This broadening effect was made possible by savoir-faire and versatility that have revealed themselves to the world as the essence of the Italic way of aggregating naturally, without having to resort to coercion.

But how can this aptitude be described in just a few words, if not as a sharing from below of values, attitudes, and behavior; a way of moving, doing business, eating, feeling, experiencing art, fashion, design, taste, beauty, and pleasure? It is an entirely particular and irreducible way of being a community in the various environments all over the world in which Italicity has integrated itself, showing its ability to represent the world in a glocal relationship that goes well beyond the old horizon of national divisions.

So then, where, if not in the connective potential of digital technology, can we find the privileged space for the aggregation of Italics?

It's a short step from this to recognizing the importance of the network.

The great themes — peace, international relations, dialogue among cultures, positive debate among religions — are increasingly being discussed and re-launched through this new virtual reality.

And thus, the Italic community can assume a fundamental role on the Web in constructing an acephalous global network, conducted by shared values and behavior that create aggregation and can produce real, measurable advantages in the prospect of a better world.

Networking

If the zero space and time of the Internet have an infinite potential for development, it is easy at this point to observe how Italicity is already a concrete reality (always equal and always different at various latitudes) composed of true communities. Faces, stories, singularities that were able to find different pathways for encounter.

In fact, since we began observing Italicity at work, we have realized that, for a while now, there are many online realities that, although at an embryon-

ic state and in certain cases not completely consciously, deal with and parse Italicity as best suits
them. There are hundreds of Italic communities on
the Web, initiatives that might arise through local
or personal needs, but that always end up spread-
ing and becoming a vehicle of connection.

These networks are the humus of new politics
and — why not? — could also develop themselves
even further as an expression of functional sectors
such as tourism, fashion, sport, food, or design.
This wake-up call to the challenges of Italicity even
passes by way of a bet: to ensure that these junctions recognize each other as virtual agoras, places
of representation and encounter, of sharing what is
happening in the various Italic communities scattered throughout the world.

In this optic, the networks will have to be more
than just instruments of virtual relations; above all,
they must be subjects that reveal the connections
between concrete realities, whose interests, aims,
and goals can enter into contact and constitute
themselves in communities. Thus, not networks, in
the sense of simple supports to network communication, but systems of regular exchange, able to as-
sist and develop functional sectors. These are the
subjects with a real interest in exploiting the possibility of inhabiting and using a system of global relations, but also of exploiting the synergy that de-
rives from intertwining it with other functional
networks. I am thinking of a fashion network, or a

food network, of the strategic advantages that could derive from interlacing and reciprocal stimuli with other networks such as those of tourism or finance.

But there's more. The intensification of network communications will have to be accompanied by a flowering of increasingly numerous "official places" in which the Italics of the world can physically encounter one another, so that the shared culture to which they aspire can be nourished and act as an identitary and strategic engine. This will be the space for a renewed associationism and, later, for a renewed diplomatic policy. All this will be possible only if, right from the start, these aggregating platforms can be created to function not merely as virtual places where communications and their resulting relations are limited to an instantaneous "appearance on the Web," but as vivid and vital aggregating instruments, continuously enriched by organizational, cultural, and political contributions: spaces through which we can catalyze the Italic community life.

The creation of an Italic digital system of this kind, universally and freely accessible, permeated with news and information, would represent an exponential leap in clarity and transnational penetration.

Language And Languages

But what language should all this occur in?

The topic is not minor.

According to the old logic, citizenship must have a corresponding language, which reinforces the national identity of the people who live in a state.

In a world of nations, political identity and cultural identity overlap and find in the so-called national languages not only the means to create internal cohesion, but also a way to affirm themselves abroad. In other words, language as an instrument of aggregation and dominion.

But in the fluidity of the glocal world, the intersection between language and territory is becoming increasingly hazy. I remember the time I was returning to Italy after having spent nine months studying at Cornell University. Onboard the *MS Vulcania*, I was sharing a cabin with two true-blue "paisanos." One of them asked me a question that left me dumfounded: "How do you say pizza in Italian?" Obviously, to him, pizza was an American word and he was asking an Italian to translate it for him: an incredible inversion of language, culture, and territory!

This is why I always reply in the affirmative when I am asked if Italicity should go beyond speaking only in Italian. The new concept of community that transcends borders must, in fact, transcend them linguistically, too. This does not mean that the Italian language should not be defended on a cultural level. But if this defense is conducted by considering the language an instrument of political communication, then it is in contradiction to what has been said to this point.

The more a language is felt to be a "shared" language, the more it will develop its ability to aggregate. This is one reason why Italics, in view of becoming a worldwide community, should not adopt Italian as their only instrument for communication.

What language will Italics speak?

Easy: The new actors of this future awaiting to be written will be multilingual.

After all, to some extent, Italians have always been multilingual; until just a few years ago — and under certain aspects, still today — they have always spoken their dialect, as well.

Today, the global Italic community speaks not only Italian and its dialects, but at least English and Spanish, as well. And it also communicates in other languages. For example, body language. Not by chance, there is a *Dictionary of Italian Body Language*.

In the debate over the future difficulty of how the various linguistic realities will communicate on a global level, the shared opinion is that English, despite its myriad contaminations, has assumed the role of lingua franca. Already now, by producing information in English, Italics can communicate with British, American, and Canadian Italics without necessarily being hindered by the fact that they haven't made the effort to learn Italian. The same can be said if the choice falls on Spanish, another global language spoken throughout the world, in general, and among Italics, in particular. In any case, should choices of this type be made, it would be counterproductive to ignore the unofficial languages of spoken dialects — which maintain their importance and vitality in associations of emigrants and their relations with their regional and municipal places of origin — since they, too, are an expression of widespread glocalism.

But, as opposed to English or Spanish — linchpins of true geopolitical strategies such as economics and political relations — Italian has the great advantage of never having been a language of power, with the exception of the late-Fascist imperialistic endeavors. On the contrary, Italian is not a language that is imposed, but rather one that is chosen.

History has shown that each time Italian was a language of election, of choice, it has played a role of recognized prestige, whereas it always remained marginal whenever the attempt was made to impose it as a political language.

This might be the reason why Italian has so often been incorporated, integrated, and metabolized in art, music, literature, culture, landscapes, and products and lifestyles of the "Italian way of life." From a language that was to a certain degree forced into the constraints of a presumed "purity," slowly but surely it also transformed itself into a precipitate that can be found in the rich variety of the languages of art, fashion, and design.

These topics came strongly to the fore during our fieldwork when, for example, we were faced with the case of Switzerland, where Italian plays a particular role and the Italic paradigm has opened new prospects for Swiss quadrilingualism. In fact, a heated cultural-political debate is ongoing in Switzerland, and the problem of defending this quadrilingualism is increasingly pressing.

In Switzerland, as opposed to other parts of the world, Italic culture is the vector enervating the country with hybrid contributions (derived from a blending of "Italianism" and "Ticino-ism"), orienting the country positively toward a prospect of multiculturalism.

There is another element that cannot be ignored. Italics have always possessed and freely used a variety of languages, thanks to their natural predisposition for technical and functional expressive forms, each time bringing to life a jargon that is constantly updated.

In order to become a reality, the new community will need to produce a more organic system of languages that should be aggregating and not rigidly bound by the use of a single language. Thus, in the case of networks, the glocal society has presented us with a growing number of vernaculars tied to particular functions: transversal, hybrid languages that cross several territories (both physical and virtual) and distance themselves more and more from the linguistic politics of states and territorial institutions. These vernaculars are increasingly organizing themselves to serve specific functions: science, the markets, finance, politics, law, but also fashion, food, music, and all the way to body language, as we have seen. "Network" languages, so to say, the offspring of the mobility of things, people, and signs. In other words, the offspring of such an encounter that characterizes our century: the one between functional globalization and identitary localism.

The Italic communicative space is, thus, much richer and vaster than the one that regards the Italian language alone.

If a country reasons by language, a community that transcends borders, such as the Italic community, reasons by vernaculars and redirects to itself and to its own identity the many great potentials of a hybridization that is constant and significant, even from the linguistic point of view.

Naturally, art and literature cannot remain indifferent to these stimuli. There is now an Italic literary vernacular that stands apart from Italian, not just for the language it uses, but also for the stylistic features it recurs to. This Italic expressive ability can be found, for example, in American authors of Italian origin like John Fante and Don DeLillo whose rhetorical methods and references can clearly be traced back to an Italic matrix. Let me stress this point: Italic, not Italian. It isn't a coincidence that I chose DeLillo as an example. When questioned, the author has always denied feeling more or less Italian. It would be quite a different matter if he were asked how Italic he and his writings are!

We should also ask, then, to what degree filmmakers like Martin Scorsese or Quentin Tarantino have drawn from Italic (in this case "American Italian") values and styles.

To encourage the aggregation of Italics, the challenge is to combine the novelty of the Italic condition − living in a glocal world − with the parallel novelty of the vernaculars themselves, which should be the most apt to embody the communicative needs of a fluid world and the best equipped to navigate the new highways of global communication. They connect people who decidedly do not want to feel they belong first of all to a nation, but who instead experiment with the historical opportunity to be part of a "community of feeling" or "of practice." These global communities are developing more and more and are crisscrossing the world with the transversal energy typical of those who are shaping the future.

Italicity: The Potential Of A Virtual Plaza

But in order for all this to happen, this fabric of relations must take on the form of an ideal territory. A territory which somehow interweaves with that of the "network of networks," the Internet.

This is already taking place, in part. This encounter is deepening the system of networks involved and designing something very similar to a real territory, in its functionality.

It is a digital territory, not a physical one, but it could lend itself to supporting a surreptitiously political one. I believe I have identified it, and I call it the "ItaliCity." It is an electronic plaza for an Italic city which dares to recognize its cultural ancestry in the "ideal city" of the Renaissance, but does so with an eye on the future. It offers itself as a place of debate, exchange, and contrast — also political — for growing glocal aggregations. A place where Italics can freely interact in the best and most direct way possible. This is where, for example, the Italics of Buenos Aires could communicate, express opinions, and do business with the Italics of New York. Who, in turn, could do the same thing with the Italics of Sydney, without necessarily passing by way of Rome or Milan.

Like every free and open membership, the ItaliCity should offer vast opportunities for contact by taking on the task — and this is a priceless quality in the era of globalization, when many traditional values are questioned and emptied — of strengthening that Italic identity we are addressing.

I don't think of the ItaliCity as something to be considered in vague or abstruse terms: it's true that, concretely, an Italic plaza is generated each time and anywhere one Italic recognizes another Italic and establishes a relationship with him or her. But what is certain is that the development of a community dimension of this type, although multifaceted, can offer countless motives of attraction: Just think of the possibilities for associationism, sharing (cultural or functional), market opportunities, political ones. Extraordinary effects could be generated for the millions of Italics throughout the world, many of whom have already created strong ties with each other. To wake up to the Italicity within the ItaliCity will mean initiating a constant interaction with the opportunities offered by the new global community. Which, I repeat, already exists and, without a doubt, does not need to be created, but properly structured in order to live in the agora of this new polis.

The Italic Media: A Global Newsroom On The Threshold Of The Web 2.0

In this overview of experiences and theoretical reflection, could we possibly neglect the problems involving the new media?

Of course not! On the contrary, it is a vital question.

Already back in the 1990s, at the time of my involvement with Assocamerestero, the basic question was whether or not there was a media system that could be defined as Italic. In conducting this research, the approach adopted was primarily inspired by Gutenberg: We concentrated primarily on an analysis of the printed media, and initially, only on Italian ones.

But it didn't take long before we realized that this approach ran the risk of limiting the analysis to the exclusively national dimension, in opposition to the spirit of our activity. Thus, the field of investigation was extended to the Italic media scattered throughout the world. Already in 1994 there were approximately four hundred news media outlets that could be defined as Italic; ten years later, there were almost seven hundred. In 2011, further updating brought the number up to eight hundred (among those regularly surveyed). Of these eight hundred outlets, four hundred fifty-five were printed publications: newspapers (fewer than ten) and, above all, weekly and monthly publications, and the like. There were two hundred seventy-four radio outlets and "only" forty-six television outlets: generally, radio and TV programs inserted by broadcasters who also dealt with other types of programs. But there were also numerous independent radio stations.

Comprehensively, in 1994, the majority of the Italic media were located in Europe. But there were also many in Latin America and North America. Australia, South-East Asia, and Africa that lagged behind. And there was a negligible number of them in China and the rest of Asia.

"Global editing staff" was the expression coined by Niccolò d'Aquino, who conducted the survey, to indicate the total number of journalists of these media outlets: Approximately two thousand people. Without a doubt, it was a special type of editing staff because, for instance, they didn't give much importance to the language. At the time of the study, 54% of the journalists — roughly half — still wrote and spoke only in Italian, but 41% of them were bilingual, meaning they made use of the language of their new territory of adoption, primarily English or Spanish. And 5% only used the local language. This means that 46% — almost half — of the Italic media did not consider Italian as the sole and indispensable instrument of communication. And the percentage was growing.

It was, thus, a very widespread phenomenon, and perhaps the moment has come to realize its potential: The present-day crisis of newspapers and the media is, in this sense, a warning.

As d'Aquino pointed out, this number should have "gotten the antennas quivering of the most alert insiders in news and advertising, not to mention politics." But in fact, almost nobody's antennas started to quiver. A great opportunity was wasted. Because, combined, these media — printed newspapers, online papers and websites, radio and television programs, blogs, etc. — have an enormous ability to create a network, especially on the threshold of the Web 2.0.

Online socialization and the enormous impact of the new technologies regarding the very essence of information can open new doors and reveal innovative opportunities for those who want to create an identity.

But how can we efficiently structure these subjects, potential flag bearers of Italic awareness and information?

As I mentioned, we must work on various fronts.

The first is the Web, the net-like space that the Italic media should elect as their privileged territory of aggregation.

The second regards the nature of the news, which in order to represent, Italics should have a personal recognizability; in substance, it should be "Italic news."

And the third front takes us back to the topic of language.

It must be stressed that when we speak of communication, we must distinguish between traditional communication, managed from above, and a polycentric open source. What I wish for the Italic media is anything but a system with a single center that broadcasts news and information. On the contrary, it must be an innovative system, which must be both polycentric and unitary, and it must have completely new organizational aspects.

This is why the network dimension must be fostered. Only this dimension can help affirm the values of Italicity in those who are not of Italic origin. In other words, only if the information of the Italics in the world can assume the characteristics of networkability (i.e., if it can broadcast and receive news regarding all the Italic realities, and in this way fertilize the community of reference with Italic facts and happenings) will this a-territorial global community be able to connect itself.

Italics, as potential inhabitants of a community, already need to recognize themselves in the news media that represent them, in this way deducing their own nature as a community from a flow of events — the news about them and their actions. If communication is able to overcome territorial borders, Italics involved in the news industry — no longer tied to national logic but inspired by the mobility so well illustrated by Bauman's wasps — can bank on the success of their means and their product, and consciously produce Italic information.

And this brings us to the second point. An Italic system for exchanging news, with its own code and rules, represents a crucial passage. Naturally, it must be constructed. The desired qualitative leap regards the acquisition of awareness, the capacity for recognition: "This news regards me as an Italic," or "it involves other Italics like me." Cohesion among Italics would be reinforced by picking up Italic news items from other media of the same genre, creating an inclusive and viral circulation.

Of course, a fundamental part of Italic communication will continue to be played by the dozens of Italian media outlets abroad. They can renew their role and their raison d'être in Italicity, developing their own form of Italic media, as junctions of communication and the representation of Italicity in the many glocal communities of Italics.

As such, this media system must speak all the languages of the Italic communities. What makes a news item Italic is, in fact, its content, certainly not the language in which it is communicated.

In synthesis, the immense and inimitable cultural patrimony of Italicity will have a promising future only if it can parse itself as an aggregation of Italics. And if it will entrust its propagation to new actors, equipped with international and global knowledge and mentalities, overcoming the increasingly evanescent and anachronistic national clichés; using the instruments of technology; always keeping in mind the language of origin, but also fearlessly promoting Italicity as a community able to deploy itself through traditional media and also on the Web, on the hundreds of Italic news outlets and social network profiles, ever more involved in a flow of communications that is proudly Italic.

4.

BUSINESS IS (NOT ONLY) BUSINESS

At this point in our story — of action and reflection, life experiences and the desire to understand the times we live in — we must return to that first binding factor we encountered at the beginning of this book and whose supremacy now appears more evident: business.

I have always been convinced that economics should be the chosen field in which to construct this hoped-for "Italic civilization," at least in an initial phase. What better field for observing Italicity at work, if not the world of business, that apparently neutral environment guided, on the whole, by pragmatic and practical reasoning?

As the saying goes, business is business.

And yet it was in that very dimension of economics and business that, many years ago, I first glimpsed the new socio-political dynamics in action. And not by chance. In fact, the world of business is where the implications of the transformation from "Italianism" into "Italicity" (which was already under way in its historical progression) first became evident. Already back then business was revealing itself as the catalyzer of processes which foster hybridization, because it embodies the fundamental dimension of interest in exchanges, linked with the dimension of values. Through the filter of economics, the Italic business community was the first community to recognize Italicity as an aggregating factor. At the time, within a network that was already very global, the decidedly Italic "shared system of interests and values" was also manifesting itself as a further, extremely important element of aggregation for people whose origins or ancestry were not Italic, but who felt themselves as such (or aspired to feel and represent themselves as such). In Italicity, a precious factor was discerned for constructing markets and exchange opportunities, able to coincide, or at any rate converge, with people's own values and interests.

Today, we can say that the Italic business community has matured a shared economic and manufacturing vision, and is able to address a market that is to all effects global. It has understood that the consumers of the globalized world have little interest in whether or not products or major brands are tied to the institutional and political dimension of a country; it has even realized that the previously mentioned "Italian sounding" phenomenon can be considered an Italic characteristic as well, radiating positive factors of attraction.

As we have affirmed, Italicity propagates values and interests that are to a certain degree hybrid. Naturally, this hybridization can conflict with very precise interests, and this also involves products.

In any case, in my opinion, it is important that we pinpoint who actually possesses the added value generated by hybridization. For example, who should receive the added value of Parmesan, which is an American re-elaboration of a source code (in this case of Parmigiano Reggiano) composed of specific styles, tastes, values, and interests? Parmesan is neither a typically American nor a typically Italian product. It is something else.

This apparent contradiction, which characterizes products created by hybridization, can be set to rights by membership in a higher level of synthesis, Italicity. It cannot be denied that these products have a market. The fact that their name "sounds" Italian is a highly attractive element for consumers because they associate it with the tradition of Italic excellence — in this case gastronomic. Furthermore, it seems that many of these products are made by second — or third — generation Italians, who thus regain a sentimental relationship with their culture of origin, albeit through the economic dimension.

Not by chance, even the president of Slow Food, Carlo Petrini, in a video message broadcast during a major convention in Philadelphia in 2011, emphasized the role played by this ability to create hybridizations founded on quality and savoir faire: "People talk a lot about Made in Italy. I think it's important that we highlight how much more wide-spread and rooted the Italicity of our culture is."

Thus, I believe that the hybridization of products should be read in a positive light, when it is combined with a search for standards of Italic excellence and quality, because it reflects a rare ability to parse a productive patrimony (which we have called a "source code") in products that can easily be placed in various societies and markets.

But the key element, able to spark interest and adhesion, is instead the universe of values which, more or less explicitly, has inspired these products. German cars are not bought throughout the world simply because they are German but because, regardless where they are produced, they reflect a combination of values, the precipitate of a mentality that hinges on precision, quality, and efficiency. In the same way, Italic products — including the "Italian sounding" ones — seduce consumers because they are vehicles of an imaginary of fantasy, taste, savoir vivre, and savoir faire that originated in Italy but has now been propagated and can be produced by the entire Italic "population."

Toward Italic Chambers of Commerce

This is clearly a historical innovation that could define an era: Today, this combination of Italic people's values and sensitivity has outstripped the relevance of flags or passports and is making headway in business, the epitome of the globalized world.

And all the more so because an Italic business community potentially already exists.

What now needs to be done is to determine its structure. At present, it has an initial organizational nucleus, albeit in an embryonic stage, that is represented by two components: the network of Italian Chambers of Commerce abroad, and the system of multinational companies that can be defined as Italic. The world isn't only dotted with multinational companies registered in Italy; there is also an entity formed of businesses, registered throughout the world, whose cultural orientation is predominantly Italic.

The truly mixed Chambers of Commerce, whose Italian partners number less than half of the total, are already widely frequented by the Italic business community, alongside traditional national institutions (ICE, the National Institute for Foreign Commerce; the Economic Sections of the Italian embassies; the financial leaders of Switzerland, Canton Ticino, and the Republic of San Marino).

But the Italic business community exploits the second component — the multinational companies — in ways that have less to do with ongoing business and more with cultural or political aspects.

The economic dimension of the worldwide business community has rapidly embraced the opportunities offered by the techno-scientific innovations of the global world, making use of the languages of the Web and the social media, and the opportunity to move rapidly anywhere in the world to create a network. This has generated communities based on the sharing of practices and interests, where the economic dimension intertwines with the dimension of values and identity. Thus, new relational realities are increasingly taking shape: transversal networks — as opposed to borders and territories — that are organized around functions (finance, media and communications, manufacturing and professional sectors, research, etc.) and rendered cohesive and coherent through flexible bonds.

As we have seen, the Italic business community has no problem identifying values, styles, and languages that characterize the Italic way of doing business. There are activities and sectors in which entrepreneurs of Italian origin have always stood out: fashion, food, design, architecture, film, and all those activities in which the tradition of artisan craftsmanship and the concept of "a job well done" have historically characterized the "Italic genius."

I think these potentials, so evident in worldwide business, must be the starting point for launching a system of authentically Italic values as an important factor of aggregation and affirmation of Italicity throughout the world. The Italic business community could thus exploit its ability to create networks, taking advantage of an affiliation that goes beyond the dimension of culture and values, so essential in an economic world in which knowledge and relations are an added plus enhancing the ability to stand out.

But in order to develop this process of aggregation, the Italic business community must have at its disposal transnational spaces and forms of representation for interests that can transcend (without ignoring) the logic of territories and borders, and instead more consciously aim at valorizing the patrimony of knowledge, customs, and abilities that the already mentioned third category shares.

And this is where the Italian Chambers of Commerce abroad can come into play. In the world of mobility, functional institutions play a leading role in every trans-territorial pathway defining how any activity is carried out: from financial activities to cultural and educational ones, from those of science and research all the way to business dealings.

Historically, the Chambers of Commerce have always been able to embody the type of institutions which the Italic economic dimension needs.

Today, there are roughly twenty-five thousand businesses revolving around eighty Italian Chambers of Commerce abroad. These businesses are Italian, local, and mixed. And an increasing number of sub-communities tends to prefer relations with entrepreneurial subjects that share affinities of customs, values, and business styles. The most recent data indicates that approximately 80% of the businesses associated with the Chambers of Commerce are foreign, proof that, in fact, foreign companies and professionals are truly interested in doing business with companies associated with the sphere of Italicity. Overall, this trend is strongly on the rise.

If the Chamber of Commerce system wants to respond to the need for representation and services of the glocal world and the new protagonists of business, then it must also elaborate a new approach, inspired by the idea of Italicity.

This is why the moment has come to accelerate the passage to Italic Chambers of Commerce, or rather, Chambers of Commerce that can increasingly present themselves as interlocutors and representatives of all those realities which, by their very nature, cannot help but express themselves in a global dimension, even though they might be solidly rooted in a particular territory.

The objective of the Italic Chambers of Commerce (a condition which naturally does not entail renouncing also being Italian Chambers of Commerce) should be to offer Italics specific instruments and services, contributing first of all to the birth of a communications system conceived within a network-based and not a centralized logic, and to the creation of shared opportunities, such as initiatives, encounters, and markets. Hence, Chambers of Commerce which, besides carrying out their organizational duties, are the ideal place to express a different entrepreneurial identity and to animate a plurality of interconnected actors and multidirectional and complex synergies. This is obviously a new type of activity for the Chambers of Commerce, to act as mediators between businesses and a new statehood to better validate and develop the Italic business community.

As far as I am concerned, I believe that in today's glocal world, it is decidedly more effective if Italics present themselves as bearers of the "Italicity" brand and not only of the "Italian-nation" brand, still burdened with old stereotypes. If the Chambers of Commerce abroad can undergo a similar evolution, they will find themselves with a market numbering millions of people: a much bigger and also friendlier market. The consumers of the globalized world should, in fact, be more influenced by the association of products or brands to the universe of values they aspire to, rather than to the institutional and political dimension of the country in which these products are made.

The birth of Italic Chambers of Commerce opens new possibilities: immediate access to information, news, and updates on new products, normally not available in a static context; the opportunity to communicate and collaborate through discussion forums, chat rooms, and other instruments of work; the circulation of products or services through preferential channels. Another element of added value that is not to be underestimated is free open data research in shared databases. And these are only a few examples.

Thus, the Italic business community should learn to give value to the businesses that belong to it, in Italy and anywhere in the world, by offering them cues about the needs and expectations of consumers, direct and immediate feedback on market conditions, the means to promote the development of new products and businesses, and access to Italic markets throughout the world.

Obviously, we must grasp the complexity of this process, which presents crucial problems, such as the proper form of legitimation and safeguarding of these products, which have apparently shifted from some parameters and qualities inherent to an approach that is merely territorial or "of origin." It is obvious that we are referring to products such as Parmesan, or palenta. But in the future, this receptiveness to diversity and the ability to generate hybridization will permit the Italic business community to maintain an important role and will guarantee a market and a space where it can affirm itself in the world.

This is why I believe we must act today, without further delay, to start transforming the Italian Chambers of Commerce abroad into Italic Chambers of Commerce.

The first Italic Chamber could be founded anywhere, in New York, Beijing, Caracas, Lugano, or Milan. A few Chambers of Commerce — in Brussels, New York, London, São Paulo, Zurich, and other cities — have already shown interest.

A first step toward the birth of the Italic Chamber of Commerce could be to propose that the network of Italian Chambers of Commerce throughout the world begin presenting themselves not only as Italian Chambers abroad, but also as Italic ones.

Naturally, it is not merely a question of terminology. But it is a change that I do not hesitate to call ontological. In fact, an Italic Chamber of Commerce is, in its essence, different from an Italian Chamber of Commerce abroad. The idea of functional poles at the service of expanding the Italian peninsula's business throughout the world must be transcended and substituted by that of organisms whose duty is to facilitate the aggregation of the business of Italic companies, wherever they might be. Thus, the work of these Chambers of Commerce is not unidirectional, but rather, acts like a network.

For example, the Chamber of Commerce of Ticino has chosen to join the Belgian-Italian Chamber of Commerce, thereby establishing a direct contact with that reality and proving its readiness to perceive the relations between functional subjects in a new way that is inspired by the ability to create networks.

To accelerate the Chamber system in an Italic key — and this must be stressed — means to consider business not merely as an activity dedicated to manufacturing and exchange, but rather as it presents itself today: the first receptacle of the many stimuli generated by techno-science, functionality, organization, and management. And, as such, directly connected with other dimensions, in particular the political dimension.

#madebyitalics

Every new aggregation, every new homeland, needs new inspirational symbols which reflect it and can be sent out into the world.

For the Italic business community, which represents the economic dimension of the nascent Italic reality, the epochal passage will be from "Made in Italy" to "Made by Italics," a concept which transcends the former one, transferring to the world of business the same relationship that is taking shape between Italicity and Italianism.

"Made by Italics" products are and will be those products that are manufactured and exchanged worldwide by the Italic business community; these goods and services hinge on Italic quality and characteristics, and are authentic interpreters of the appeal of the Italicity brand. But "Made by Italics" will also describe the relations, cultural exchanges, and strengthening of identity and aggregations that will take place within the Italicity network, online and offline.

My hope is that the Italics of the world will make this formula theirs and relaunch it along the broad range of their own relational networks. In this way, rather than remaining confined to the realm of professional insiders, it may immediately project itself outward, pouring itself into the flow of communications like a phenomenon that is destined to come to the fore in the transnational imaginary.

My wish is that thousands of Italic entrepreneurs will embrace the symbol by using it on Twitter and on the Web as a hashtag (#madebyitalics) accompanying their activities and business communications, as a symbol of a new affiliation that can be summarized and communicated in a formula that reveals an economic world of relations and exchange, able to act as a pioneering interpreter of how the nascent Italic community is being constructed.

In fact, in an increasingly hybrid and interconnected world, the supply and demand for an Italic market is already taking form. And this is what we propose to call "Made by Italics." Starting tomorrow, we can work on transforming the existing structure and redesigning it according to the glocal gusts of wind that are lashing the markets and the very identity of tens of millions of individuals.

Perhaps no other network like that of business can contribute to binding together the Italics, who are potentially already alert to our call.

New Actors For New Networks: The Makers

We must bear in mind that this same glocal wind is already strongly affecting how traditional business is conceived and conducted; and it is raising the curtain on another historical caesura: the so-called "third industrial revolution." The maker revolution is proposing criteria of aggregation that can no longer be traced back solely to technology, but also to creativity, and thus to culture and values, as well. Business could prove to be a powerful aggregator in this revolution.

The capitalism of knowledge and the possibility offered by 3D printers to pass directly from "the bit to the atom" — to borrow the motto coined by the director of MIT's Center for Bits and Atoms, Neil Gershenfeld — are shifting the perspective from Taylorism to the "prototype as a product," or rather, to the maker movement. In fact, the drastic reduction in production time made possible by 3D printers is profoundly changing the very essence of artisan craftsmanship and the relationship between designer, "backer," and consumer. It is the end of a concept of work embodied by Charlie Chaplin in Modern Times, the workman of the 20th century; it is the end of the limit imposed when designers do not possess the necessary means to manufacture; and it is calling into question the roles of capitalist and manager. The lag between project and creation, between an idea and its realization, has been radically reduced. Many of the crucial traits of Italicity are recognizable in this counter-culture of the makers. The true key element of this challenge is the authentic bottom up character of this reality, which emerges from the bottom and propagates itself on the global network.

This challenge sees these two worlds (these two "hives," distinct yet somehow similar) coming into direct contact on the field of the economics of beauty. This contact is made possible by the fact that an Italian designer or artisan, like an Italic one (as we have seen by tracing the historical pathway of Italicity), is the bearer of the millenary knowledge of our particular, anthropological savoir faire — so closely bound to beauty — which has innervated centuries of artistic, musical, and cultural production.

This conviction found its validation in the experience of the Giannino Bassetti Foundation's project Innovating with Beauty, a precious opportunity for encounter and debate between Italian artisans and standard-bearers of Silicon Valley. The project was created to broaden the knowledge and manufacturing ability of the custodians of our knowhow through collaboration with the people who are writing the newest chapter of the digital revolution. Innovating with Beauty: Technology plus Beauty.

Thus, among the many possible alternatives, the first outlines of Italicity are taking shape: the creation of "communities of practice" that hybridize each other, with exceptional repercussions on employment for young people and the ability to anticipate the consumer demands of tomorrow, which are destined to focus increasingly on the personalization of products and, thus, of markets.

Remember Bauman's wasps and the ease with which they passed from one nest to another? Let us try to behave with the natural and millenary wisdom of those insects. Let us integrate two vanguards — technology and the ability to create beauty — in order to generate a new one that is ready for the future.

It is in fields like this that Italicity can properly measure itself within the nuclei of global encounters, terrain for experimenting with its potential and its ability to hybridize, innervate, and create products, mobility, employment, and new global pathways.

5.

ITALICITY AS A POTENTIAL POLITICAL SUBJECT

An Appeal To The Elite

But who will be the new protagonists of this epochal revolution? And what will bind them together? Every process of aggregation we have dealt with until now — culture, communications, language, media, business — calls for everyone involved in the organizational and functional framework of civil society to do their part.

But in this discussion, a central role must be played by the elite.

In fact, in order to aggregate and completely fulfill its potential, Italicity needs to express a ruling class of its own to inspire, unite, and guide it.

This is not a new phenomenon. Through the centuries, the presence of Italics has not only been a story of humble migrants who moved from less favorable environments toward universes of hope and redemption. It is also a story of the elite, such as representatives of the worlds of finance and diplomacy; leading exponents in art, fashion, design, and research; our intelligentsia.

Initially, Italicity must find a space for its embodiment within this elite. The Italic ruling class will

be called on to fulfill — instinctively or purposeful-
ly — this new community aggregation's prospects
of birth and its management.

When I speak of the elite, I mean representatives of the world of media and the network of intellectuals; Italian associations abroad such as religious and missionary orders (Combonians, Jesuits,
Scalabrinians, Salesians, etc.); the diplomatic, cultural, and linguistic networks; and, naturally, the
network of business.

It is obvious that the term 'elite' can no longer
only call to mind somewhat classical figures in the
collective imaginary: as I already explained, we must
also think of the makers, the new generations of
programmers, the innovators of startups, artisans.

All these people are asked to see themselves as
invested with a role that now evokes more than just
the value of their origins; it also asks them to offer a
conscious contribution to give Italics a clear idea of
their Italicity.

Already back in 2000, I was fully aware of the
central role the elite play in the Italic world community's process of aggregation and affirmation.
That is when I decided to create a committee which
would expand the debate in order to bring to the
surface all the potential energy of the Italic issue,
gradually tracing a pathway of analysis and reflection, and pinpointing which element of Italic aggregation transcends all juridical, nationalistic, and
territorial acceptations. I extended my invitation to

intellectuals, academics, entrepreneurs, representatives of the third sector, and free thinkers. My idea was to create a permanent discussion forum for what I was still calling the "world in Italian," a forum open to intelligent people willing to pursue the goal of giving visibility to the Italic universe and evaluate the merits of and the opportunities for concrete projects. I named the committee "Pro Italica," and, not by chance, the first official definition of the Italic community was formulated during a meeting at Palazzo Giureconsulti in Milan on July 18, 2000, and was later inserted in the document Il Mondo in Italiano. Alla ricerca di una koine italica [The World in Italian. In search of an Italic koine]. That meeting sanctioned the passage from the concept of the world in Italian to Italicity.

Today, looking back, I can see that we have come a long way since then. Moreover, the topicality of the idea at the basis of that encounter is increasingly vital.

Naturally, others are called on today to carry the message; the task of involving others must be exponential.

Who am I referring to? Who is my target?

We have already drawn up a provocative list in these pages, whose declared ambition is to be a pathway to the future and a call to arms. Let's return to that list and add a few more names.

I am thinking about people like Mario Draghi, Sergio Marchionne, Diego Picentini, Carlin Petrini,

Giorgio Armani, Gay Talese, and Quentin Tarantino. And I could add many others by including other fields of endeavor: from fashion to sport, from the world of culture to that of the economy.

But I am also thinking of many presidents of our Chambers of Commerce abroad; of representatives of the worldwide Catholic network, many of whom have collaborated with me over the years; of Catholic associationism which, in its various forms (from the already mentioned Scalabrinians and Combonians to its own media networks, such as the online monthly *Messaggero di Sant'Antonio*), has conserved its aggregating power in a globalized world.

So then, how should this enormous potential be mustered and mobilized in order to serve our purpose? This topic is not only open; it is of primary importance.

We are asking our elite to draw inspiration not solely from the Italian flag (naturally, they may continue to do so, if they wish) but to present themselves in this new specific role, whose valorization has a precise objective: the construction of a new global subjectivity. We are all called upon to pursue this objective, to join ranks with those who have already embarked on the journey. And they are legion!

It is a leap in perception, if you will: from a negative to a positive, from the defense of Italianism to the construction of Italicity.

Exhorting the elite to assume this responsibility, spurring them on to form a network that can pursue the goal of increasing the presence of Italicity in world history: This must not be a mirage. The Anglo-Saxons and the Hispanics have already achieved this goal in part. Now it's our turn.

The Challenge Facing All Italics

Therefore, the process to affirm Italicity's identity exists, and it is making headway. Perhaps more through heterogeneous impulse than through conscious design, more as an open source than as a top-down movement. Plus, there is still an element of risk that can only be overcome through leadership. And this is where the elite come in. The Italic debate, its ability to inspire new political synthesis, can assume historical relevance only if our elite focus on it and, finally, provide it with a long-term strategy.

It is not simply an economic question. Instead, it is the much more complex and multifaceted need to respond to the provocations of our time.

Some of you might remember that Apple computers were the first to eliminate floppy disk slots. The reason was simple: Steve Jobs had foreseen the extinction of those supports, years ahead of time. And this is precisely what we need to do: We must start looking to the future with more than just an eye on the impulses of the present; we must also anticipate the macro-events, the new synergies and networks that are already guiding the distant future.

In conclusion to this line of reasoning, we must now lift the veil on the most recent difficulties of a world in which — as we have often repeated — history no longer involves only national populations, defined as such by state or imperial membership, but also new glocal aggregations, defined as such by the strength of their value-based, functional, and political ties, making them susceptible to progressive institutionalization. For example, large multinational companies.

After all, even countries and empires achieved their institutionalization through gradual processes. As Edgar Morin and Mauro Ceruti pointed out in their essay *La nostra Europa* [Our Europe], "Right from the start, the European Union defined itself as a project and not as a territory; it presented itself as a political entity, not as a geographical one; it outlined its borders following successful negotiations with its candidates for membership and not on the basis of declarations of principle regarding the final demarcations of European civilization."[1]

And this is precisely the essence of these reflections.

Because of the ongoing process of globalization, the nation-state is gradually losing its supremacy in its response to the needs of new memberships, as

---

[1] Translator's version.

well as its leading position in policies regarding security, defense, and economic development.

Sabino Cassese expressed this concept very well in his book *Chi governa il mondo?* [Who Is Governing the World?].

From its position as a dominant monopolist of legitimate violence, the nation-state, after losing its sovereignty, was long ago forced to fragment itself into a constellation of functions that operate on various levels and are inspired by principles of networkability and subsidiarity. In short, it has increasingly become more like a functional unit within a composite universe of networks, local and regional powers, authorities, agencies, international organizations, associations, clubs, and cults.

As a result, we must no longer look to the nation-state for an identity we can share in. In fact, the ongoing process of glocalization has deeply influenced not only the individual identity, but the collective identity as well: this is the crux of the existence and significance of national states, which expressed and characterized themselves in the concepts of citizenship and membership.

Arnold Toynbee had foreseen the historical role of civilizations when he proposed a model of interpretation tied to their major phases — rise, consolidation, decline. He was without a doubt ahead of his time. This is one reason he was disregarded, in the uncontested primacy of nation-states and their national populations.

But today his thinking is very up-to-date.

Samuel Huntington, with his hypotheses of the risks inherent to a world of "civilizations," returned to Toynbee's argument. Obviously, Huntington did so by referring to potential clashes that seem completely foreign to both Toynbee's approach and to the central theme of our Italic proposal.

It is better, more opportune, to start from the supposition that only the dissolution of the old international system can open a space in which we can constitute new identities and politico-institutional affiliations that better respond to the logic of today's global structure: above and beyond any problems related to a "clash of civilizations."

Whereas, until now, a great deal of history (in particular revolving around states) has been the result of top-down reasoning and actions, the techno-scientific digital revolution and conditions of mobility seem to have produced an inversion in political history able to spark the idea of a new, burgeoning statehood which does not present itself in a hegemonic way but instead configures itself as a reality that has somehow been formed from below.

To many Italics, this is a true, de facto, transnational citizenship.

The most important effect of these innovations is, in fact, that they call for new aggregations that are open, functional, and hybridizing; not closed and confined in order to remain territorially distinct. Of course, they, too, need identity, subjectivity, and organization, but these will only be found by searching outside Westphalian tradition, with its borders, completed homelands, national ideologies, and wars won or lost. They must be sought, not without effort, in the formation of institutions that are new because they are different and, as such, call for the creation of new homelands, of new symbols.

After all, when today's Anglo-Saxons, the heirs of England's grand political school, speak of the Commonwealth, and Hispanics speak of the Hispanidad, they are doing this exact same thing. They are not following new hypotheses of empires or kingdoms, but new forms of institutionalization, able to welcome and develop their traditions and present-day prospects for aggregation. And when the United States will see every possibility for a personal (albeit new) empire vanish, and China will realize the danger it is running by chasing after one — both at the risk of abandoning their very different historical-cultural traditions — what else will they be able to do but convince themselves that the world of the nation-state is irremediably finished and that the glocal world demands different approaches?

Thus, new large communities such as the Italic community, commonwealths in the making, can prove to be a great resource in the contemporary world, since they are made of transnational networks crisscrossing and interconnecting the planet.

After all, this gradual transcending of merely national logic is already sparking concrete political processes. For example, the construction of Europe, with the case of the euro and the Schengen Pact, but, paradoxically, also of the caliphates.

The challenge facing the heirs of Westphalia — but first of all the Italics — is to harvest the political potential of this process. This challenge can be best faced by those, like us, who are already well aware of the need for a new idea of politics, as a consequence of the presence of a new polis.

This is the pulsing heart of our discourse to Italics: here, at the crossroads between the end of the old, international system of states and our reflections on a new, glocal statehood.

Our modern times, with the deep crisis affecting states, have long evoked the need for an idea to substitute the concept of nation and nationalism. The psychological and existential wealth challenged by glocalization compels the political coexistence — in keeping with the original European project — of the many identities inherent to the new forms of aggregation, obliging them to cohabit with national states, but transcending them, toward the top and toward the bottom, in order to meet the needs of glocalism.

The Idea Of A Commonwealth

Therefore, our challenge is to wake up to the condition of Italics and interconnect our subjectivity (both ancient and new) with a different state-hood.

And it is in light of this challenge that we Italics, all the world over, must choose to redefine, talk about, and organize ourselves in order to consciously present ourselves as builders of a new form of commonwealth that links Italian history and Italic history. We are spurred on to do so by the great success of the Italic presence in the world today. A success which, once more, offers us the opportunity to lay the foundation for a different world order.

As in every form of "living" culture, tradition is something that can be rediscovered in contemporaneity.

To Italics, territoriality is an aspect that cannot be confined within the borders of the modern state. We are universalists: to us, every local dimension of origin is projected, with new linguistic and social idiosyncrasies, onto a global level, perhaps thousands of kilometers away, but always in a world-wide dimension. The Italic culture has always taken form on this global level. We inspired Rome, the universal Church, and the Holy Roman Empire; we attained our maximum expression during the Renaissance, the migratory and hybridizing experiences of the peninsula's inhabitants before the Unity of Italy, the fantasizing period of modernism and Italian nationalism, and finally, at the turn of the millennium, with the advent of globalization. And this is still the case today, at the dawn of an emerging commonwealth that is beckoning millions of people throughout the world to its hive and to its values.

Our culture is the result of the worldwide diffusion of people to whom hybridization has always been an active process. People who are, therefore, natural candidates to construct their own "hive" around completely new social and cultural experiences; who, in this phase of history, are beginning to surface and constitute themselves in phenomena of membership with exceptional economic and identitary potential. People for whom this prospect is a new phase in their own centuries-long pathway, which must evolve into a political pathway.

This world community is learning from what it has seen and what it is seeing now; and hence, it is able to respond creatively to the present challenges.

Rather than asking us to renounce our various national traditions, it is able to aggregate and finalize them for current objectives; it can look at the present and prepare itself for the future, rendering the purely national aggregations more fluid in order to better seize the potential of the new localisms and functionalisms that glocalism is introducing. All this to express a type of political subjectivity to be exerted in the prospect of a new statehood, in which the relationship with techno-science, information, the new communitarianism, and innovative ways to produce, regulate, compel, and defend can be profoundly reconsidered.

Thus, to construct a new Italic subject means to call upon the millions of people on the five continents who are interested in this mission. Men and women whose linguistic, institutional, and political identification might vary greatly but who have a sufficient number of shared values and interests, allowing them to feel and affirm that they are in search of a new identitary and civil hive. As we already noted, the inspiration informing this container must be neither solely Italian, nor solely Italian-American, Italian-Australian, or Italian-Argentine, and the like. It must be a new glocal identity that flanks the one defined by a passport or territory of residence, without necessarily coming into conflict with it. The challenge is to grasp this subjectivity, organize it in the glocal world, and elaborate a proper institutional order.

Can political science help us in this undertaking?

I am firmly convinced it can.

As long as it accepts a radical rethinking of what has been and still is the mainstream consideration regarding states, of course.

In fact, I do not believe that the needs of the political organization of Italics and Italicity can be served by a state that is still characterized by the prevailing concept of it: a state that can be defined as "an organized community living under one government. States may be sovereign" (in the words of a "sacred" text of the Web culture, Wikipedia).

A great portion of our discourse has been dedicated to the assumption that the glocal world has changed not only the nature of power and the way it is exercised, it has radically changed the function of territory as a predominantly organizing space in political relations. And above all — and in particular — it has changed the way populations belong to it, thanks to the mobility that is replacing "putting down roots" as the dominant condition of the appurtenant populations. I repeat, to us, this old way of organizing power by entrusting its management to the idea of a state appears, by and large, outdated.

So then, what?

In our search for a possible alternative, we reflected on the term "commonwealth." This term, in its true acceptation, not only contains a different conception of power — it hypothesizes a search for "wellbeing" (wealth) rather than a search for order through stability. But above all, it presumes a different idea of the relationship between politics and power: from the revolutionary and, therefore, bottom-up relationship of a Cromwell, to the structurally despotic one of a French king, born such by the grace of God.

Considerations such as these strengthened our conviction that, whereas the political container of Italianism had been the national state, Italicity will need a very different kind of political container: and I have in mind something closer to a commonwealth than simply a larger state.

To help us define the generic organism (the current interpretation of the term refers to the Commonwealth of Nations, or rather, the present organization of fifty-three member states of the old British Empire, ruled by Queen Elizabeth II), we turned to the considerations of Lorenzo Ornaghi in his book *Il concetto di interesse* [The Concept of Interest]. Here, Ornaghi, reflecting on Hobbes's thinking, wrote that "it is significant that in the 16th century, the lexeme 'commonwealth' (in which 'wealth' is the abstract form of 'weal,' a lexical loan translation of the Latin 'bonum publicum') was commonly used to indicate the 'political body,' whereas before, this term had been used to denote — contemporaneously and indiscriminately — both the 'political body' and 'wellbeing.'" Of course, there can be no doubt that Italicity will not be replacing the state any time soon. Rather, it will oblige the states in which it takes root to progressively gain awareness of the expectations which feed it and to respond to them.

As opposed to the case of Great Britain, Italicity does not have an imperial structure in its past; therefore, it must look to the concept of the commonwealth and its fluid institution. Only in this way can Italics, within the global system, gradually acquire political recognition for the centers of organized cohabitation in which they live (and in this manner, subsidiarily foster proximity to the different needs of the Italic communities on the various continents). All this in a growing awareness of increasingly being able to belong to that new transnational political organization which we are encouraging the existing Italic communities, both large and small, to peacefully construct.

A New "Risorgimento"

This challenge is difficult yet possible because — it is worth repeating — social systems are behaving in a new way in our glocal world.

Open source modalities rendered possible by digital technology are, in fact, changing many assumptions regarding the old way of conducting politics.

We have already stated that we consider the characteristics, the distinctive traits of Italicity — that broad range of values, and ways of feeling and behaving — like a true source code everyone can contribute to. Thus, we are experiencing the Italic source code like an open source commonwealth, able to freely inspire the individuals and the actors of the future to adopt, evolve, change, and relaunch it in a new manner, according to the degree to which each individual has made it his or her own.

The role of open sources in the digital revolution is well known. And above all, to our ends, their ability to create communities, to produce bottom-up convergences of intention and action in a group of people of shared but heterogeneous origin is evident. From 1998 — the year the term was coined — to today, open sources have played a key role in the free circulation of information, making it possible to form communities of interest and practice. In synthesis, they have contributed to molding the contemporary mindset, setting free creative abilities and exchanges of ideas, in a way that permits a quality leap for all users and is not tied to economic availability alone.

The open source is an ameliorative logic par excellence: Users can evaluate and test a program, discovering bugs, defects, and weak points, and eliminating them. Vice versa, they can identify the strong points, too, enhancing those characteristics with greater potential.

It must be said that, obviously, there will be no "copyright" on Italicity and that, on the contrary, its emergence must be spontaneous and widespread. In any case, what fascinates us is the mechanism: the possibility of free access to a "source code," to make it ours, to modify and develop it, transforming an idea like this into a political fact on a global scale.

To have a source code (which is what we are trying to delineate here) at our disposal permits programmers and other advanced users to modify the program as they please, adapting it to their own needs.

At this point, we are calling on Italics to reflect on all this, so they can best grasp in which process the hoped-for historical subjectivation of Italicity can be concretely consolidated.

It is not simply a case of ensuring that the ties we have glimpsed converge in a new historical-political design, but rather, of knowing how to adopt Italicity's source code according to people's personal inclinations and becoming actors in writing it. On an individual basis, in the perception and construction of one's identity as a global and glocal citizen. On the professional and business front, by recognizing the Italicity of one's own interlocutors and valorizing it as a keystone of and deep-rooted conduit for interaction with others. On the political front (or as regards the near future, on the pre-political front), recognizing that the Italic communities of practice and feeling of today and tomorrow prefigure the outlines of a transnational subject which will progressively gain awareness of its political weight and, thus, of its resulting needs, demands, responsibilities, and margins of growth.

In conclusion, a final bit of advice.

There will be no Italic commonwealth without something that history has made the keystone of our era: informational collaboration.

This collaboration means giving visibility to our pathway and that of the other Italics who will enter the fray. It means products manufactured for Italic markets, media able to recount Italic happenings, opportunities for cultural encounters, exchanges of views and perspectives, in both the offline and the online worlds. And it means clearly labeling these initiatives as Italic.

The deep significance of these pages — to awaken the Italics of the world to the possibility of liberally drawing on a combination of values and shared practices — can only occur in an environment of widespread informational collaboration.

Not every modification of open source software leads to improvements; in the same way, the near future of Italicity, too, must reckon with the fact that it will encounter a few blind alleys. If, on the identity front, membership without the need for mediation is within everyone's reach, the Italic evolution of the various systems we have discussed (from the media to business and political action) is an obstacle course that will require time and more than a little trial and error. Just like in the development of open source software, blind alleys are a part of the process. In fact, they are a vital part of it, indicating more clearly which pathways can be followed and which ones are premature or simply unproductive. In short, the program must be tested, and every possible contribution will enrich it. The point is to free the potential of the Italic being in every direction. To inaugurate an era of exploration, with the construction of the "Italic civilization" as the Pole Star of our navigation.

6.

YOUNG PEOPLE, OUT TO CONQUER
THE ITALIC HOMELAND

I want to dedicate the last pages of this book to young people, for they are the ones who will decree the success, or not, of a world community that is in the process of being constructed.

I have spoken of identity, media, business, and commonwealth: the four terrains for which Italicity might become a determining, evolutionary factor for millions of men and women throughout the world.

But in order to call itself effectively complete, Italicity needs one more thing: a soul.

It needs strong aspirations, individual pathways characterized by the desire to make and to change certain rules of the game in order to nourish, animate, and give it that "extra something" which can make it unique and unrepeatable.

I asked myself, what purpose can Italicity serve?

My reply was, to help people recognize themselves in each other, not by banally looking beyond the differences, but in the fruitful and hybridizing dialectic between diversity and similitude that bonds a North American Italic with one from South America, Australia, or Europe.

It is necessary to parse in an Italic key a potentially global market that retraces and strengthens those pluri-identitary practices that can bring together the Italic global communities of the world.

And, finally, its purpose is to find the warmth of this New Homeland we want to inspire people to create over time.

"I feel Italic." I would like to find this sentiment on the Web, on Facebook and Twitter profiles, in the blogs and on the websites of people who read this book. But also, and above all, I would like to find this declaration in the individual pathways of today's twenty- and thirty-year-olds, who are setting out — in their own country and in the world — with all the ambition of young people who want to construct a satisfying and fulfilling future for themselves. In today's crisis-burdened Italy with its sky-high youth unemployment, when the discussion turns to young people, a bugbear begins to loom: the mantra of the "brain drain."

Instead, our advice is, "Let them go and feel Italic anywhere in the world."

I am firmly convinced that this invitation for people to recognize themselves in Italicity isn't only the most encouraging context for these initiatives, virtuous circles of professional mobility, both incoming and outgoing. Part of its innovative reach also consists in calling into question certain stifling figures of the imaginary, such as the brain drain.

The prospect that considers a return to the homeland as the only way to forestall the loss of social capital belongs to the old paradigm of the nation-state, in which the concept of homeland coincides with that of borders. Instead, today, values are de-territorialized, societies are liquid, identities are negotiable and multiple, and so is the sense of homeland. It is with this political intuition that I invite young people to gaze on the world, in the hope that the institutions of our country will also be willing to observe it from a similar perspective.

A young Italian who relocates abroad no longer moves within the old paradigm, and the option that he or she remains abroad is not damaging; it is neither an irreplaceable loss, nor a draining off of value from one country to another. On the contrary, it is an important opportunity. Our young people are wasps, off to pollinate territories that aren't necessarily foreign, not irremediably alien, and they will, in turn, hybridize themselves. In Metternich's day, the homeland had to be refounded by transcending that famous "geographical expression," and thus by conquering territory. Today, this is no longer the case.

Italicity is able to attract the Italian brain that is "in flight," just as it can attract the brain of the grandchild of an Italian emigrant in the United States or in Argentina, who speaks English or Spanish and not Italian, and who identifies strongly with the society in which he or she grew up. And through Italicity, every departure and every arrival brings added value to the hive of this world community in ferment.

After values have been de-territorialized and Italic communities disseminated throughout the world, the costs and benefits will be summed up using a new type of math: the one applied to the global field lines that will increasingly interconnect the Italics of the world.

I want to say this to young people: Be a determining part of this new polis, this pluri-identitary citizenship that offers an added dimension to your actions. Be American, Brazilian, Australian, Italian, Argentine, homebodies or globetrotters, makers or students, professionals or the managerial class of tomorrow. But know how to construct your new Italic world. Since you are Italics, feel yourselves protagonists of a grand historical design: Don't make Italicity a cultural prospect, make it a political subject.

To Italics everywhere, I say: Your successes and your achievements will bring value, identity, and membership to this new homeland, to the soul of this transnational "civilization." The more you feel it yours, the more you will help create it.

I want to wake Italics up to the pursuit of this proposition.

To awaken in them an awareness of their existence.

To exhort them to assume responsibility in the great transformation our glocalizing world is undergoing.

To render them, as such, a subject of history.

Italics, let's wake up!

BIBLIOGRAPHY

Accolla, Paolino, and d'Aquino, Niccolò, ed., *Italici. Il possibile futuro di una* community *globale*, incontro con Piero Bassetti. Milan-Lugano: Giampiero Casagrande, 2008); English translation, *Italici. An Encounter with Piero Bassetti*. New York: Bordighera Press, 2008.

Appadurai, Arjun, *Modernità in polvere*. Rome: Meltemi, 2001.

d'Aquino, Niccolò, *I media della diaspora: giornali, radio e televisioni dell'Italia fuori d'Italia*, preface by Piero Bassetti and Susanna Agnelli. Rome: Presidency of the Council of Ministers, Dept. of Information and Publishing, 1994.

d'Aquino, Niccolò, *Annuario dei comunicatori italici nel mondo*. Turin: Media Press, 2005.

d'Aquino, Niccolò, *Annuario dei mass media italici nel mondo*. Turin: Media Press, 2005.

d'Aquino, Niccolò. edited by), *La rete italica. Idee per un Commonwealth. Ragionamenti con e su Piero Bassetti*. Rome: Italic Digital Editions, 2014.

Bassetti, Piero, "L'Italia mondiale. Il mondo in italiano," *Limes*, 4 (1998), 307-314.

Bassetti, Piero, "Il mondo in italiano oltre la cittadinanza," *Politica internazionale*, xxviii, 4 - 5 (2000), 101 − 104.

Bassetti, Piero, *Globali e Locali! Timori e speranze della seconda modernita*, edited by Sergio Roic´. Milan-Lugano: Giampiero Casagrande, 2001.

Bassetti, Piero, "Italicita: globale e locale," in Paolo Janni, and George F. McLean, eds., *The Essence of Italian Culture and the Challenge of a Global Age*, proceedings from the seminar *The Council for Research in Values and Philosophy*. Washington, D.C.: Catholic University of America [CUA], April 2002, Washington, D.C. 2003.

Bassetti, Piero, "I giovani del mondo globale. Domande e opportunita," in Segafreddo, Luciano, and Traini, Armando, *Le nuove generazioni in un mondo globalizzato di fronte alle sfide dell'integrazione*. Padua: Emp, 2007.

Bassetti, Piero, "Glocalizzazione e finanza," *Notiziario della Banca Popolare di Sondrio*, 106 (2008), 45-47.

Bassetti, Piero, "Glocalismo, fenomeni e linguaggi dell'italicita nel mondo. Chi puo dirsi davvero italiano?," *Messaggero di Sant'Antonio*, 1129 (September 2010).

Bassetti, Piero, *Preface*, in Macrì, Fabrizio, *Oltrefrontiera*. Vicenza: Caosfera, 2011.

Bassetti, Piero, and d'Aquino, Niccolò, "La Svizzera italiana nella sfida glocal," in Mazzoleni, Oscar, and Ratti, Remigio, eds., *Identita nella globalita. Le sfide della Svizzera italiana*. Milan-Lugano: Giampiero Casagrande, 2009.

Bassetti, Piero with d'Aquino, Niccolò, *Italic Lessons. An Ongoing dialogue.* New York: Bordighera Press, 2010) (bilingual edition).

Bassetti, Piero, and Janni, Paolo, eds., *Italic Identity in Pluralistic Contexts, Toward the Development of Intercultural Competencies,* executive summary and extracts from the seminar *The Council for Research in Values and Philosophy.* Washington, D.C.: Catholic University of America [CUA], April 2003, Washington, D.C., 2004.

Bauman, Zygmunt, *Globalizzazione e glocalizzazione.* Rome: Armando, 2005.

Bauman, Zygmunt, *Capitalismo parassitario.* Rome-Bari: Laterza, 2009.

Bauman, Zygmunt, *L'arte della vita.* Rome-Bari: Laterza, 2009.

Bauman, Zygmunt, "Migration and Identities in the Globalized World," *Philosophy & Social Criticism,* xxxvii, 4 (May 2011), (Los Angeles-London-New Washington D.C.: Sage Publications Ltd), 425-436.

Beck, Ulrich, *La societa cosmopolita. Prospettive dell'epoca postnazionale.* Bologna: il Mulino, 2003.

Bitjoka, Otto, *Legittime aspettative. Il cammino dell'immigrato nella nuova Italia,* preface by Piero Bassetti, afterword by Pino Polistena. Turin: Claudiana, 2014.

Caon, Fabio, *Dizionario dei gesti degli italiani. Una prospettiva interculturale.* Perugia: Guerra, 2010.

Caritas italiana, Fondazione Migrantes, *xxiii Rapporto immigrazione. 2013*. Todi: Tau Editrice, 2014.

Cassese, Sabino, *Chi governa il mondo?* Bologna: il Mulino, 2013.

Castellin, Luca Gino, *Ascesa e declino delle civilta. La teoria delle macro-trasformazioni politiche di A.J. Toynbee*. Milan: Vita e Pensiero, 2010.

Con la scrittura superiamo il cultural divide, interview by Luca Romano with Michela Murgia, The Huffington Post, http://www.huffingtonpost.it /luca-romano/scritturasuperiamo-cultural-divide_b_5901116.html .

Corradi, Consuelo, and Pozzi, Enrico, "Il mondo in italiano. Gli italiani nel mondo tra diaspora, business community e nazione," preface by Piero Bassetti, *I quaderni di impresa e Stato*. Milan: Chamber of Commerce of Milan, 1995.

Friedman, Thomas L., *Il mondo è piatto*. Milan: Mondadori, 2005.

Globus et Locus. Dieci anni di idee e pratiche (1998-2008) (Milan-Lugano: Giampiero Casagrande, 2008.

Huntington, Samuel P., *Lo scontro di civilta e il nuovo ordine mondiale*. Milan: Garzanti, 2000.

"La lingua italiana è un patrimonio e uno strumento geopolitico," interview by Nicolò Locatelli with the Undersecretary for Foreign Affairs Mario Giro, *Limes* (October 2014), http://temi.

repubblica.ßit/limes/la-linguaitaliana-e-un-patrimonio-e-uno-strumento-geopolitico/67427.

Ligi, Gianluca, *La casa saami. Antropologia dello spazio domestico in Lapponia.* Turin: il Segnalibro, 2003.

Micelli, Stefano, *Futuro artigiano. L'innovazione nelle mani degli italiani.* Venezia: Marsilio, 2011.

Morin, Edgar, and Ceruti, Mauro, *La nostra Europa.* Milan: Raffaello Cortina, 2013.

Ornaghi, Lorenzo, ed., *Il concetto di interesse.* Milan: Giuffrè, 1984.

Ortino, Sergio, *La struttura delle rivoluzioni economiche.* Bari: Cacucci, 2010.

Robertson, Roland, *Globalizzazione. Teoria sociale e cultura globale.* Rome: Carocci, 1999.

Roić, Sergio, ed., *Il percorso dell'italicità.* Milan-Lugano: Giampiero Casagrande, 2006.

Sassen, Saskia, *Le citta nell'economia globale.* Bologna: il Mulino, 2003.

Savinio, Alberto, "Lo Stato," in Nigro, Salvatore Silvano, ed., *Dopo il diluvio. Sommario dell'Italia contemporanea.* Palermo: Sellerio, 2014.

Sen, Amartya, *Identita e violenza.* Rome-Bari: Laterza, 2006.

Silvestri, Giorgio, *I media della diaspora italiana. Dal bollettino al blog.* Madrid: Marenostrum, 2009.

Tirabassi, Maddalena, *I motori della memoria. Piemontesi in Argentina*. Turin: Rosenberg & Sellier, 2008.

Tirabassi, Maddalena, and del Pra', Alvise, *La meglio Italia. Le mobilita italiane nel xxi secolo*. Turin: Accademia University Press, 2014.

Toynbee, Arnold Joseph, *Le civilta nella storia*, compendium of D.C. Somervell. Turin: Einaudi, 1950.

"Un fil rouge fra Made in Italy e Italicita," interview with Stefano Micelli, in *Globus et Locus*. March 2012), http://www.globusetlocus.org/Press/Interviste_Glocal/Un_Fil_Rouge_Tra_Made_In_Italy_E_Italicita.kl.

The Italics Project

In recent years, the association Globus et Locus has set itself the task of fostering the aggregation of Italic communities and promoting their cultural and institutional subjectivity, crafting a multifaceted fabric of relations, creating and organizing encounters, collaborations, and project and operative synergies with important institutional and cultural interlocutors throughout the world, also involving exponents of the business community and the media.

But this process of aggregation was also self-propaga-ting, and it was fueled both autonomously and thanks to the cooperation of various actors in worldwide Italic communities (including foundations, regions, territorial bodies, universities, businesses, etc.). One of the most important is the system of Chambers of Commerce, which, as an expression of interests and structures supplying services to the world of business on a glocal level, represent an example of functional transnational aggregation.

Initiatives

The concept of Italicity was analyzed through the promotion of and participation in various initiatives, throughout the world, on topics regarding culture, the media, business, and language. The following is a concise list of the major initiatives, in reverse chronological order.

2015

March-December, "Italic Network. The map of italic cities in the world as new approach to foreign markets for italian design products", research realized in collaboration with Chamber of Commerce of Monza e Brianza.

December 3, London, presentation of *Svegliamoci Italici!* by Italian Culture Institute.

December 2, Pavia, *Quality and transparency of the market. Lessons of history for future rules,* event by Chamber of Commerce of Pavia.

November Project "Italic design Thinking", project promoted by Scuola Politecnica of Design, in collaboration with Globus et Locus and Fondazione Giannino Bassetti.

November 27, Melfi, presentation of *Svegliamoci Italici!* book in Fondazione Nitti.

September 29, Monza, presentation of *Svegliamoci Italici!* book in Monza, Novaluna Association.

October, *Despertemos Italicos! Manifiesto por un futuro glocal,* the book of Piero Bassetti has been published in South America by Cyngular publishing house.

September 18, Bari, presentation of *Svegliamoci Italici!*, at Fiera del Levante.

September 6, Milan, presentation of *Svegliamoci Italici!*, during the event Senza perderci di vista, in Festa of Democratic Party with Eugenio Marino, National responsible for PD of Italians in the World, and Fabio Porta, President Italians in the World Commettee.

July 23, Milan, presentation of *Svegliamoci Italici!* book in ISPI, during the event, "Reset Italia. Un progetto globale per il paese (ed. Guerini)", with Ambassador Giancarlo Aragona, ISPI, Giovanni Brauzzi, Ministry of Foreign Affairs, Luigi Tivelli.

June 23, Bergamo, presentation of *Svegliamoci Italici!*, with Major Giorgio Gori, Sen. Gilberto Bonalumi and Vice director of *L'Eco di Bergamo*, Franco Cattaneo.

June 17, Milan, event Glocalization and Italicity, promoted by Assocamerestero and Globus et Locus, in Palazzo Giureconsulti.

June 9, Lugano, presentation of *Svegliamoci Italici!* book, during the event "Form Italophonia to italicity", in General Consulate of Italy. Woth Ambassador Cosimo Risi, Consul Marcello Fondi; Remigio Ratti, Carlo Cattaneo Association.

June 6, participation of President Piero Bassetti to "Otto e Mezzo", broadcast, in order to speak of his book and of the concept of Italicity.

May 28, Milan, presentation of *Svegliamoci Italici!* in Istituto Lombardo, Brera Academy.

May 15, Milan, presentation of *Svegliamoci Italici!* in Wired Next Fest, with Andrea Illy.

May 15, Turin, presentation of *Svegliamoci Italici!* in Turin Book Fair, with Sergio Chiamparino, President Piedmont Region and Luca Ubaldeschi, Vice Director of La Stampa.

April 16, Milan, Fondazione *Corriere della Sera*, presentation of the Book *Svegliamoci*

Italici!, by Piero Bassetti, with Ferruccio De Bortoli, Corriere della Sera Director; Fabio Finotti, Director of Center for Italian Studies, University of Pennsylvania; Giuseppe.Recchi, President Telecom.

March, 13, Brescia, Confartigianato, presentation of the Book *Svegliamoci Italici.*

March 14, *Svegliamoci italici! Manifesto per un futuro glocal* (Marsilio) by Piero Bassetti, by.

28, Udine, University of Udine, presentation of the Book *Svegliamoci Italici!*, by Piero Bassetti.

2014

October 22, Florence, States-General on the Italian Language. Participation at the round table *Italofonia: prospettive dall'estero.*

October 19, Ancona. Participation at the 23rd Assocamerestero world convention.

July 15, Naples, Italian Institute for Philosophic Studies. Presentation of the book *La rete italica. Idee per un Commonwealth.*

May 9 — 10, Basel, Rathaus/Grossratsaal-Universität Basel. Globus et Locus is one of the sponsoring bodies of the international convention *L'italiano sulla frontiera. Vivere le sfide linguistiche della globalizzazione e dei media.*

March 31, Milan, Eni Foundation. Meeting of the Assocamerestero Advisory Board (of which Piero Bassetti is a member), entitled *Dal Made in al made by. Nuove sfide per la promotion italiana.*

2013

November. Collaboration on *Italica*, a new column in the web journal *La voce di New York*, directed by Stefano Vaccara. Publication of an interview with Piero Bassetti on the concept of Italicity (*Nel nuovo mondo glocal, protagonist della storia anche 250 milioni di italici*).

November 10, Monza. Participation at the 22nd Assocamerestero world convention *Expo 2015: un'opportunita e una sfida per le imprese e il territorio.*

October 28. Piero Bassetti sends a video message to the yearly assembly of the Italian Scholars and Scientists of North America Foundation (ISSNAF).

October. Research project on the topic of contemporary migrations and new mobility from Italy (with a focus on the North-West), developed by the Altreitalie center of Globus et Locus and published in the book edited by Maddalena Tirabassi and Alvise del Pra', *La meglio Italia. Le mobilita italiane nel xxi secolo*, Turin: Accademia University Press, 2014.

September 20, Turin. Participation at the convention for the 28th anniversary of CRI, the Italian-speaking radio and television community.

April 3 — 5, Philadelphia, University of Pennsylvania. Participation at the international convention *Italicity. The Languages of Italy in the United States between Tradition and Innovation*, organized by AISLLI (the international association of Italian language and literature studies) and by Globus et Locus, in close conjunction with the Italian Embassy in Washington, D.C. and the Consulate General in Philadelphia.

2012

November 10, Milan. As president of the Talea project's committee of honor, Piero Bassetti participates at the General Assembly on Immigration event entitled *Il merito mette radici*.

October 20, Turin. Participation at the convention for the 27th anniversary of CRI, the Italian-speaking radio and television community.

August. Collaboration begins with the Venezuelan entrepreneur Alfredo D'Ambrosio to create an online platform dedicated to Italic aggregation: Italicos.com.

July 7, Rome, Montecitorio, Sala della Mercede. Participation at the presentation of the book by Guido Tintori *Il voto degli altri*, about the Italian vote abroad.

2011

September — December. Collaboration begins with the customer care office of the company Sea, to fine-tune a questionnaire for Italic passengers of Sea in order to produce a mapping of how Italicity is perceived.

September. Publication in the journal of the Belgian-Italian Chamber of Commerce *Infoitalie* of an interview with Piero Bassetti regarding Italic Chambers of Commerce.

September 19, Turin. Participation at the convention for the 26th anniversary of CRI, the Italian-speaking radio and television community.

September 14, Lugano. Participation at the event *Il futuro è glocal!* on the topic of the business relations between Italy and Switzerland, promoted by the World Trade Center of Lugano.

August. Creation of the Italicity community's Facebook page, to stimulate the online aggregations of Italics.

July 15, Udine, Università degli Studi. An event dedicated to the theme *Valori identitari e imprenditorialita*. The encounter is an offshoot of the FIRB-Ministry for Education, University and Research project, promoted by the organization "Friulani nel mondo" and by a network of Italian universities.

July 12-15, Turin. *Summer Academy 150* of the Altreitalie Center, on the occasion of the 150th anniversary of the Unity of Italy.

April 27, Brussels, Belgian-Italian Chamber of Commerce. Participation at the event *Fare Business con gli italici. Il ruolo delle camere di commercio italiane all'estero*, dedicated to the business opportunities within the Italic network.

April 15-16, Philadelphia, University of Pennsylvania. Participation at the convention *From the Unity of Italians to the Unity of Italics. The Languages of Italicity Around the World*, promoted by AISLLI and Globus et Locus, together with the Italian Embassy in Washington, D.C. and the Consulate General in Philadelphia.

April 9, New Jersey, New Brunswick-Rutgers University. Participation at the 42nd convention of the Northeast Modern Language Association (NeMLA). An encounter on the topic *Italicita: identita, linguaggi e aggregazioni nel mondo piatto*.

2010

November 22, Zurich, Italian Chamber of Commerce for Switzerland. Participation at the event on the topic *L'Italia compie 150 anni, e gli italiani? L'identità italiana nell'era della globalizzazione*.

November 5-6, Lugano. Participation at the convention for the 25th anniversary of CRI, the Italian-speaking radio and television community.

July 5-7, Turin. *Summer Academy* of the Altreitalie center.

June 4-12, Camaldoli. Participation at the seminar of the Ethnoland foundation, organized as part of the Talea project.

May 27-29, Florence. Participation at the convention *Piazza delle Lingue dell'Accademia della Crusca*, dedicated to the topic *L'Italiano degli altri*.

April 20, New York, Calandra Institute. Piero Bassetti sends a video message to the presentation of the book *Italic Lessons*.

2009

December 3-5, Philadelphia, University of Pennsylvania. Participation at the convention *Languages, cultures, identities of Italy in the world*, promoted by AISLLI.

May 22, Florence. Participation at the convention *Piazza delle Lingue dell'Accademia della Crusca*, dedicated to the topic *Multilinguismo, pluriap-partenenza e italicita.*

2008

November 12, New York. Participation at the round table *Italy-city. The Internet Generation. Global, Local or Glocal?* promoted by i-Italy, Casa Italiana Zerilli-Marimò, John D. Calandra Italian American Institute, Bordighera Press, Consulate General of Italy in New York.

November 12, New York. Participation at the event *The U.S. and the European Union: Views on the Present and Future*, promoted by The Italy America Chamber of Commerce.

2007

November 16-17, Alessandria. Participation at the 3rd conference *Piemontesi nel mondo*, organized by the Piedmont Region, Regional Council, and Regional Committee, along with local institutions.

Publication of the blog Italicando.

2006

October 21-27, Lecco. In collaboration with Assocamerestero, coordination of the 25th world convention of the Italian Chambers of Commerce abroad.

August, radio program *Dante Vagante*, made in collaboration with RTSI and CRI, the Italian-speaking radio and television community.

July 6, Milan. Seminar *Glocalismo e Lingua Italiana: sfide e prospettive*, in collaboration with the IULM University foundation.

2005

June 14-15, Chianciano Terme. Participation at the 10th Summer School of the Master's Degree course in Communications and Media of the University of Florence.

June 5-7, Vilnius. Participation at the convention *Globalization, National Identities and the Quality of Life*, in collaboration with the Center for the Study of Culture and Values, Catholic University of America, Washington, D.C.

March 18-19, Fribourg. Participation at the convention *I media italici in Europa come veicolo di integrazione culturale*, organized by Mediapress under the aegis of the Ministry of Italians in the World.

2004

2003/2004. The research paper *Lombardi nel mondo*, in collaboration with Irer and the Lombardy Region.

July 31, Cividale del Friuli. Participation at the 1st convention "Friulanità nel mondo."

June 4-5, Milan. Participation at the convention *Cultural Diversity in the Perspective of an Enlarged Europe*, in collaboration with the Center for the Study of Culture and Values, Catholic University of America, Washington, D.C.

2003

October 23-24, Washington, D.C. Participation at the convention *Italic Identities and Pluralistic Contexts*, in collaboration with the Center for the Study of Culture and Values, Catholic University of America, Washington, D.C.

October 10-11, Novara. In collaboration with the Piedmont Region, a contribution to the organization of the 2nd conference of *Piemontesi nel mondo*.

A feasibility study with the Agnelli foundation: *L'Italicita e le fondazioni di origine bancaria.*

2002

April, Washington, D.C. Seminar *The Essence of Italian Culture and the Challenge of the Global Age*, in collaboration with the Center for the Study of Culture and Values, Catholic University of America, Washington, D.C.

2001

Participation in the organization of the 1st convention of Italians in the World, with the support of the Ministry for Foreign Affairs. Event: *Appunti per un programma di incontri con alcune comunita di italiani in Australia.*

For further information, please consult the website www.globusetlocus.org.

Since July 2013, the Globus et Locus web journal *Glocalism* has been available online (www.glocalismjournal.net).

Published issues:

2013/1. *Hybridity*

2014/1-2. *Feeding the Planet. Energy for life*

2014/3. *Global Cities*

ACKNOWLEDGEMENTS

This book could never have taken form if it hadn't been for the intellect, perseverance, and passion of Veronica Trevisan; the judgment and wisdom of Livia D'Anna; the expert critical contributions of Lorenzo Ornaghi, Enrico Decleva, Franco Farinelli, Fabio Finotti, Stefano Micelli, Alberto Quadrio Curzio, Remigio Ratti, and Stefano Rolando; the suggestions of Davide Cadeddu, Luca Gino Castellin, Niccolò d'Aquino, Giuliano Di Caro, Riccardo Giumelli, Jacopo Guerriero, Sergio Roic, and Anthony Tamburri; the encouragement of Pasquale Alferi, Paolo Janni, Luca Meldolesi, Massimo Russo, and Armando Sanguini; and the friendly collaboration of Tatiana Crivelli, Mario De Donatis, Renato Mattioni, Francesco Samoré, Leonardo Simonelli, and Maddalena Tirabassi.

An especially important contribution to the birth of this book was provided by Armando Verde, during the thousands of miles we flew together.

As always, Bertilla Corti was indispensable.

And finally, my sincere thanks to everyone who, in other ways, also gave me a hand.

Translation by Gail McDowell

Index of Names

About the Author

PIERO BASSETTI, Milanese, is Chairman of Globus et Locus, the Association of Institutions that analyzes the consequences of glocalization on political and social life and on institutions, and of the Giannino Bassetti Foundation, its scope being the study of "responsibility in innovation." Advisor and councilor of the Comune of Milan from 1956 to 1967, he was the first President of the Lombardy Region from 1970 to 1974 and parliamentary deputy from 1976 to 1982; Chairman of Milan's Chamber of Commerce, Industry and Agriculture from 1982 to 1997, he was also Chairman of the Union of Italian Chambers of Commerce from 1983 to 1992 and of the Association of oversees Italian Chambers of Commerce from 1993 to 1999.

CPSIA information can be obtained
at www.ICGtesting.com
Printed in the USA
FFOW03n1702190217
32548FF